American Language Hub

LEVEL 2A
Student's Book
+ access to Student's App

DANIEL BRAYSHAW
JON HIRD

macmillan education

Contents

Welcome

USEFUL PHRASES
Classroom

0.1 **A** Write the words in the correct order to make useful questions for the classroom. Listen and check.

1 repeat / please / that, / Can / you / ?
2 say / do / How / you / English / *trabajar* / in / ?
3 slowly, / Could / speak / more / please / you / ?
4 do / pronounce / How / you / that / ?
5 spell / do / that / you / How / ?
6 *excellent* / What / mean / does / ?

Dates

B SPEAK Work in pairs. Answer the questions.

1 Which months have exactly 30 days?
2 What are the days of the week?
3 How do you say the ordinal numbers 1–20?
4 What date is it today?

PRONUNCIATION
Word stress

0.2 **A** Listen and underline the stressed syllables. Then listen again and repeat the words.

happy polite amazing beautiful

The /ə/ sound

0.3 **B** Listen and underline the schwa /ə/ sound. Then listen again and repeat the words.

television magazine support campus

Third person -s endings and simple past regular endings

0.4 **C** How do you pronounce the underlined sounds? Listen and repeat. Choose the correct option.

1 works /s/ /z/ /ɪz/
2 has /s/ /z/ /ɪz/
3 finishes /s/ /z/ /ɪz/
4 played /d/ /t/ /ɪd/
5 watched /d/ /t/ /ɪd/
6 wanted /d/ /t/ /ɪd/

GRAMMAR
Tenses, structures and auxiliary verbs

A Choose the correct words to complete the questions.

1 What *do* / *does* / *are* you do?
2 *Are* / *Is* / *Can* you cook?
3 *Were* / *Will* / *Are* you reading a good book right now?
4 What *is* / *am* / *are* your parents' names?
5 Where *do* / *does* / *is* your best friend live?
6 Can you *swimming* / *swim* / *to swim*?

B SPEAK Work in pairs. Ask and answer the questions in Exercise A.

VOCABULARY
Word sets

A Look at the word sets. Cross out the odd one out. Check your answers with a partner and explain your choices.

1 serious ~~old~~ friendly happy
2 at five o'clock next to me in the afternoon on Tuesday
3 across from the bank four years ago near the school behind the library
4 egg bottle bag can
5 two years ago in a month last Friday yesterday evening
6 banana apple bread orange

Parts of speech

B Match the parts of speech in the box with the words in **bold**.

~~adjective~~ adverb article auxiliary noun preposition verb

1 My **favorite** subject is English. *adjective*
2 I **read** emails in English at work. ______
3 There are 12 students **in** our class. ______
4 **Do** you speak any other languages? ______
5 We have **a** test today. ______
6 This is my new English **book**. ______
7 Please listen **carefully**. ______

Question words

C Complete the questions with the words in the box.

How many How much ~~What~~ When Where Who Why

1 *What* 's your name?
2 ______ are you from?
3 ______ is your birthday?
4 ______ brothers and sisters do you have?
5 ______ do you know in this class?
6 ______ are you studying English? Do you need it for work?
7 ______ time do you spend studying English each week?

D SPEAK Work in pairs. Ask and answer the questions in Exercise C.

1 RELATIONSHIPS

My best friend is the one who brings out the best in me.

Henry Ford

Iñupiat friends play in the first of the winter snow, Nome, Alaska.

OBJECTIVES

- find out about someone new
- talk about different types of people
- describe someone's personality
- greet people and give personal information, make introductions
- write information about yourself

Work with a partner. Discuss the questions.

1 Who's your best friend?
2 Look at the picture. Who was your best friend when you were a child?
3 What qualities do you look for in a friend?

1.1 Breaking the ice

Find out about someone new

G question forms V people P the alphabet

LISTENING

A Complete the definitions with the words in the box.

conversation relationship successful tip topic

1 A private and informal talk between two people is a ________________.
2 A useful suggestion is a ________________.
3 When you achieve the result you want, you are ________________.
4 A subject that you write or speak about is a ________________.
5 When two or more people or things are connected in some way, they have a ________________.

B SPEAK Work in groups. Discuss the questions.

1 What is happening in the photo at the top of the page?
2 Where do people usually meet for the first time?
3 How do you usually start a conversation with someone you have just met?

1.1 **C LISTEN FOR KEY WORDS** Listen to an interview with psychologist Isabelle Ackerman.

1 What topic does she talk about?
2 What should you start a conversation with?
3 What are two safe topics of conversation to 'break the ice'?

Glossary

break the ice (phrase) to do or say something that makes people feel less shy or nervous in a social situation
politics (n) the activities of governments which control a country or area
psychology (n) the study of the mind and how it affects behavior
religion (n) the belief in the existence of a god or gods
social life (n) the time you spend enjoying yourself with friends

1.1 **D LISTEN FOR DETAIL** Listen again and complete each tip with the correct verb.

ask discuss feel give know say

1 ________________ something positive about the place or situation you are in, and then ask a question.
2 ________________ about other people.
3 Don't be negative about other people because you don't know who they ________________.
4 Ask lots of questions and ________________ lots of answers.
5 When you ________________ more relaxed, ask some personal questions.
6 Don't ________________ topics like religion or politics with someone you don't know.

E SPEAK Work in groups. Discuss the questions.

1 What did you think of the tips in the podcast?
2 What other topics are easy to talk about with new people?

GRAMMAR

Question forms

1.2 **A WORK IT OUT** Complete the questions with the words in the box. Listen and check your answers.

are did (x2) do (x2) have is (x2) were

1 What __do__ you say to a stranger at a party or a new colleague at the office?
2 ________ it OK to talk about some topics, but not others?
3 ________ you ever met someone new and had no idea what to talk about?
4 ________ you having fun?
5 What ________ your favorite band?
6 ________ you enjoy the ceremony?
7 ________ you at school together?
8 Where ________ you study?
9 ________ you have children?

B Look at the questions in Exercise A. What tense are they? Write *simple present*, *simple past*, *present progressive* or *present perfect* next to each one.

C Choose the correct words to complete the rules. Use Exercise B to help you.

Question forms

1 We use the auxiliary verb (*do, does, did*) ***before / after*** the subject.
2 We use *be* (*am, is, are, was, were*) ***before / after*** the subject.
3 We use present perfect *have* ***before / after*** the subject.

D Go to the **Grammar Hub** on **page VI**.

E Rewrite the questions with the verb in parentheses in the correct place.

1 why you studying English? (*are*)

______

2 you have any brothers or sisters? (*do*)

______

3 you ever met a famous person? (*have*)

______

4 you do anything nice last weekend? (*did*)

______

5 you like tea or coffee? (*do*)

______

6 you a late-night or early-morning person? (*are*)

______

7 who your funniest friend? (*is*)

______

8 who the first person you talked to this morning? (*was*)

______

9 you ever been to a wedding? (*have*)

______

10 what the last good movie you saw? (*was*)

______

F **SPEAK** Work in pairs. Ask and answer the questions in Exercise E.

VOCABULARY
People

A Go to the **Vocabulary Hub** on **page XVIII**.

B **SPEAK** Work in pairs. Answer the questions.

1 How many relatives do you have? How often do you see them all?
2 How many of your colleagues or other students in your class are also your friends?
3 Do you find it easy to talk to strangers? Why/Why not?

PRONUNCIATION
The alphabet

1.3 **A** Listen and repeat.

a b c d e f g h i j k l m n o p q r s t u v w x y z

A B C D E F G H I J K L M N O P Q R S T U V W X Y Z

1.4 **B** Work in pairs. Write the letters of the alphabet in the correct place. Listen and check.

/e/	/uː/	/ɑː/	/iː/	/aɪ/	/oʊ/	/eɪ/
f	*u*	*r*	*e*	*i*	*o*	*a*

C **SPEAK** Work in pairs. Look again at Vocabulary Exercise A on **page XVIII**. Take turns spelling the words.

SPEAKING

A Find out some information about your classmates. Write six questions using the ideas below to help you. Then write two more questions using your own ideas.

- ice breakers
  Hi, my name's ______. It's nice to meet you. So, …
- personal questions
- family and friends
  Do you come from a large family?
- interests and hobbies
- childhood and school
- work and study
- favorite things/places
- last weekend/vacation
  Where did you go for your last vacation?

B Work in pairs. Work with someone you do not know well and follow the instructions.

1 Stand up and meet the other people in the class. Take turns asking and answering the questions you wrote in Exercise A.
2 When you have broken the ice, sit down with your partner and tell him/her about the people you met. Was it easy to break the ice or do you need some more help?

Find out about someone new

1.2 Blogs and bloggers

Talk about different types of people

V types of people **P** using a dictionary **G** frequency words and phrases

READING

A Work in groups. Discuss the questions.

1. Which websites do you visit most often and why?
2. Which blogs, vlogs (video blogs) or video channels do you know or follow?
3. What kind of topics do you enjoy reading about online?

B **READ FOR MAIN IDEA** Read *Three of the best* quickly. Which blog sounds most interesting to you and why?

C **READ FOR DETAIL** Read again. Complete each sentence with the name of a blogger, Emma, Maria or Michela.

1. ____________ is interested in visiting people around the world.
2. ____________ has children.
3. ____________ writes about a variety of subjects.
4. ____________ has a high number of readers.
5. ____________ is interested in trying new things.
6. ____________ wants people to understand that everyone is beautiful.

D **SPEAK** Work in pairs. Discuss the questions.

1. Is running a blog a difficult job?
2. Why do these people spend so much time on their blogging activities?
3. What topic would you blog about?

VOCABULARY
Types of people

A Work in pairs. Make a list of different types of people. You have one minute.

father of two, music fan, …

B Go to the **Vocabulary Hub** on **page XVIII**.

C **SPEAK** Work in pairs. Write down the names of three people you know and describe them to your partner. Say what type of person each one is. Ask questions about the people your partner describes.

PRONUNCIATION
Using a dictionary

Macmillan English Dictionary

www.macmillandictionary.com

The *Macmillan English Dictionary* gives clear, simple explanations and real life examples showing you how and when the word is used.

A Look at this entry from the *Macmillan English Dictionary*. Match the definitions (1–5) with the labels (a–e).

1. definition
2. part of speech
3. stressed syllable and pronunciation
4. different meaning
5. frequency rating

gorgeous – definition and synonyms ★[a]

[b]ADJECTIVE Pronunciation /ˈgɔː(r)dʒəs/[c]

[d]**1** very beautiful
Mandy was there, looking gorgeous as usual.

[e]**2** very enjoyable or pleasant
The weather was absolutely gorgeous.

B Look up the following words in the *Macmillan English Dictionary*. Underline the stressed syllable and write down the part of speech and one meaning for each word.

cloud expedition positive rare

Three of the best

Blogs by Calvin Norton

With over 150 million blogs online, there is something for every type of person from the **animal lover** to the **gamer** to the **sports fan.** But, if you are looking for something a little different, here are my top three blogs.

1 Brain Pickings

Maria Popova is a **book lover**, **music fan** and writer. Her blog *Brain Pickings* is a collection of articles about history, news, books and culture. Maria is interested in reading and spends hundreds of hours each month doing research for her blog. It's an extremely popular blog and many people enjoy Maria's interesting mix of articles.

2 The Atlas of Beauty

The Atlas of Beauty is a picture blog showing beauty in different cultures. Romanian photographer, **blogger** and **traveler** Michela Noroc takes pictures of women of all ages, races and nationalities living their everyday lives. It's a wonderful collection which shows that beauty can be found everywhere.

For more interesting blogs, listen to Calvin on this week's Emma Fry Show

GRAMMAR

Frequency words and phrases

1.5 **A** Listen to an interview with Calvin Norton about another blog, *Humans of New York*, and answer the questions.

1. What is the blog about?
2. What type of people does Brandon Stanton interview?

1.6 **B** Listen and complete each sentence from the radio show with one word.

1. ______________ a week, we bring you reviews and recommendations from the wonderful world of the internet.
2. I'm ______________ out in the real world.
3. I'm ______________ at home, online in front of my laptop.
4. But luckily for us, you ______________ escape.
5. Now and ______________, a blog is so good that I just have to mention it again.
6. Stanton focuses on the lives of normal New Yorkers ______________ of the time.
7. He includes someone well known ______________ so often.
8. It's a very simple idea, but it ______________ gets boring.

C **WORK IT OUT** Write the four frequency words in Exercise B in the correct place.

Frequency words

100%
- always
- usually
- often
- 1 ______________
- sometimes
- 2 ______________
- 3 ______________
- hardly ever
- 4 ______________

0%

D Complete the frequency phrases in the table with words from Exercise B.

once twice three times	1 ______________	day week month year
every 2 ______________ often		
3 ______________ and then		
most of the 4 ______________		

E Choose the correct words to complete the rules. Use Exercise B to help you.

Frequency words and phrases

1. We usually put frequency words ***before*** / ***after*** the main verb and ***before*** / ***after*** the verb *be*.
2. We use frequency phrases ***at the beginning*** / ***in the middle*** of a sentence.
3. We also use frequency phrases ***in the middle*** / ***at the end*** of a sentence.

F Go to the **Grammar Hub** on **page VI**.

G **SPEAK** Work in pairs. Discuss the questions.

1. Would you enjoy the blog *Humans of New York*?
2. Why do you think it is so popular?

SPEAKING

A Interview each other about websites, blogs or vlogs you like. Write notes about:

- what they are about
- why you like them
- examples of interesting things on them
- what type of people would enjoy them and why

B Work in groups. Interview each other. Which ones sound most interesting?

3 Emma's Bucket List

After her father and step-father died, Emma Stewart Rigby decided to live a full and exciting life. Emma, a **mother of three**, made a list of 246 things to do before she dies and in her blog she writes about her experiences. Emma is a **people person** and gives a lot of friendly advice on life. She's also a **foodie**, and her bucket list includes unusual foods or interesting restaurants she plans to try. A great blog for ideas on how to live life to the max!

Glossary

blog (n) a website containing short articles called posts that are changed regularly
blog (v) to write short articles for a website on your opinions, interests and experiences
culture (n) activities which involve music, books and other arts
subscriber (n) someone who joins and follows a blog

Talk about different types of people

1.3 Personality

Describe someone's personality

G indefinite pronouns V personality adjectives, adjective + preposition
P word stress in multisyllable adjectives S previewing a text

READING

A SPEAK Work in pairs. Discuss the questions.

1. Which do you do more often: write by hand or use a keyboard?
2. Which do you find easier? Why?
3. What kind of things do you write by hand (e.g. shopping lists)?

B Preview the text, and then answer the questions. Use the information in the box to help you.

Previewing a text

Before you read a text, look quickly at the title and any headings, pictures or diagrams. Use this information to decide what kind of text it is, what it's about and why someone might want to read it. This will make the text easier to understand.

1. What is the text about?
2. Is it from a science paper or a popular magazine? How do you know?
3. What do you think you will learn from the text?
4. Can you trust the information in the article?

C READ FOR MAIN IDEA Read *What does your handwriting say about you?* Was your preview correct?

D READ FOR SPECIFIC INFORMATION Read again and answer the questions.

1. What is graphology a study of?
2. How do graphologists help in court cases?
3. Do all graphologists agree that there is a link between handwriting and personality?

E SPEAK Work in pairs. Discuss the questions.

1. Do you believe there is a connection between handwriting and personality? Why/Why not?
2. Is it important for children to learn to write by hand these days? Why/Why not?

What does your handwriting say about you?

Everybody has their own style of handwriting, but can someone's handwriting tell you what they are like? The study of handwriting is called graphology. Graphologists are usually involved in legal cases. They are responsible for matching criminals to their handwriting or deciding if signatures are real. Some graphologists think handwriting can show anything: what kind of job you will be good at, how healthy you are and even what kind of partner you might be happy with. If you are interested in what your handwriting says about you, check out our information.

Letter size

Small: You're probably a **hard-working** person. People with small handwriting are rarely **lazy**.

Medium: The research says you're **sensible**; you think carefully about the decisions you make.

Large: Big writing – big personality! People with large writing are usually interested in parties and social events and are rarely shy.

Letter shape

Rounded letters: Rounded letters suggest you are a **creative** person. Are you good at art or music?

Pointed letters: You are **curious**. Your favorite question is 'Why?'!

Dotting your i

Dot high over the i: The research says you have a good imagination.

Dot low over the i: You are a **well-organized** person. Are your desk and room neat?

Spacing between words

Wide spacing: You're an **independent** type and you are happy on your own.

Narrow spacing: You're very **sociable** and you need other people in your life.

Your signature

Difficult to read: You are a private person. Like your signature, you can be difficult to read.

Easy to read: **Confident** people usually have signatures that are easy to read. You know what you are good at and you don't mind telling other people about it.

Does your handwriting match your personality? Don't be disappointed with the results if not. Not every graphologist believes there is a connection.

Glossary

legal (adj) relating to the law or lawyers
spacing (n) the amount of space between things

GRAMMAR
Indefinite pronouns

A WORK IT OUT Look at the extract from the article and choose the correct words to complete the rules.

Everybody has their own style of handwriting, but can someone's handwriting tell you what they are like?

Indefinite pronouns

1 We use indefinite pronouns to talk about people or things ***so we can say*** / ***without saying*** who or what they are.
2 We use indefinite pronouns with *-body* and *-one* to talk about ***people*** / ***things***.
3 After indefinite pronouns, we use ***singular*** / ***plural*** verbs.
4 We use *'s* with indefinite pronouns for ***possessives*** / ***plural nouns***.

B PRACTICE Find and underline another example of an indefinite pronoun in the article.

C Go to the **Grammar Hub** on **page VI**.

VOCABULARY
Personality adjectives, adjective + preposition

A Match the personality adjectives in **bold** in *What does your handwriting say about you?* with the speakers below.

1 'I believe I can do anything if I try. I don't usually worry about things.' *confident*
2 'I love my job. I work a lot, but that's OK.' ________
3 'I can paint pictures, write stories and make music.' ________
4 'I plan my time carefully and I always know where to find my things.' ________
5 'I don't like work. I like doing nothing! My perfect day? Staying in bed with a pizza.' ________
6 'I like to think about things carefully before I do them.' ________
7 'I have a lot of friends and we meet and go out all the time.' ________
8 'I like learning new things and I ask a lot of questions.' ________
9 'I like to do things myself.' ________

B Look at the underlined phrases in the article. Complete the questions with the correct preposition.

1 Are you involved *in* any clubs, groups or teams? Which ones?
2 What are you good ____?
3 Who is responsible ____ doing the cooking in your home?
4 Are you happy ____ your cell phone? Why/Why not?
5 What websites, magazines or TV shows are you interested ____?
6 Are you interested ____ books and reading?

C SPEAK Work in pairs. Ask and answer the questions in Exercise B.

PRONUNCIATION
Word stress in multisyllable adjectives

A (1.7) Listen and complete the table with the words in the box.

hard-working independent lazy sensible

1 ●•	2 ●••	3 •●•	4 ••●•
		hard-working	

B (1.7) Listen again and repeat the words.

C (1.8) Look again at the article. Find the other personality adjectives in **bold** and write them in the correct place in Exercise A. Listen and check and repeat.

D SPEAK Work in pairs. Practice saying the words. Listen and check your partner's pronunciation.

SPEAKING HUB

A Work in pairs. You are going to study your classmates' handwriting. Follow the instructions.

1 Sign your name and write this sentence on a piece of paper.
The quick brown fox jumps over the lazy dog.
2 Swap papers and use the information in *What does your handwriting say about you?* to write five things about your partner's personality.

B DISCUSS Using your notes, tell your partner what their writing says about them.

Describe someone's personality

Café Hub

1.4 Hello again

Ⓕ– greet people and give personal information, make introductions

Ⓟ– word stress and intonation

My name is Gaby. I'm originally from [1]_______________, but now, London is my home. I'm a [2]_______________. I like traveling and I drink a lot of [3]_______________. I live in this [4]_______________ with Neena and Zac.

My name's Zac. I live with [5]_______________ and Neena. I'm originally from [6]_______________. I make [7]_______________ games.

My name's Sam. This is my café! I'm [8]_______________. I like food. I love [9]_______________. I live here in [10]_______________.

I'm Milly. This is my clothes store. I'm [11]_______________. I watch [12]_______________, listen to music and I read a lot. [13]_______________ a good friend of mine.

Neena here. I live here in London with my two friends, Gaby and [14]_______________. I'm a lawyer. I work in [15]_______________.

COMPREHENSION

A ▶ 00:00–02:50 Watch the first part of the video. Complete the paragraphs above.

B Write a question about each person in Exercise A.
Where is Gaby from? What does Zac do?

C **SPEAK** Work in pairs. Test your memory! Close your books and ask each other your questions from Exercise B.

D ▶ 02:50–04:27 Watch the second part of the video and underline the correct verb form to complete each sentence.

1. Neena *is* / *isn't* going to an interview.
2. Sam *is* / *isn't* good.
3. Zac *had* / *didn't have* a good holiday.
4. Zac *has* / *hasn't* asked Milly out.
5. Zac *invites* / *doesn't invite* Sam to the flat.
6. Sam *eats* / *doesn't eat* Zac's croissant.

Glossary

flat **(n) (British)** = apartment **(n) (American)**
holiday **(n) (British)** = vacation **(n) (American)**

FUNCTIONAL LANGUAGE

Greet people and give personal information, make introductions

A Complete the phrases with the words in the box.

doing going hello let's long meet (x2) what

Greeting	Reply
Say hello	
[1]__________	Hi there! / Hey!
Greet new people	
Nice/Good to [2]__________ you.	Nice/Good to [3]__________ you, too.
Greet friends	
How are you? How's it [4]__________? How are you [5]__________?	I'm good. How about you?
What's new?	Not much.
It's great to see you! [6]__________ a nice surprise!	[7]__________ time, no see.
Say goodbye	
See you later. See you soon. I've gotta (got to) go.	[8]__________ do something soon.

B ▶ Watch the video again. Check your answers to Exercise A.

MILLY

SAM

NEENA

ZAC

GABY

USEFUL PHRASES

A Match the useful phrases (1–8) with the pictures (a–h).

1. Dream job! ___
2. I love it here! ___
3. Good luck! ___
4. What can I tell you? ___
5. Come with me. ___
6. What else? ___
7. Come over to the flat this weekend. / Will do. ___
8. Here we are. This is home. ___

a

b

c

d

e

f

g

h

B ▶ Watch the video again and check your answers to Exercise A.

C How do you say these phrases in your language?

PRONUNCIATION

Word stress and intonation

A ▶ **03:02–03:34** Watch part of the video. Read out the conversation at the same time as Sam and Zac. Copy the word stress and intonation.

Sam: Hey Zac. It's great to see you. What a nice surprise.
Zac: I know. Long time, no see.
Sam: Do you want a coffee?
Zac: Sure, and a croissant.
Zac: So, how are you doing?
Sam: I'm good. How about you? Did you have a nice holiday?
Zac: Yeah. Always good to see family. What's new with you?
Sam: Not much. Same, same.

B SPEAK Work in pairs. Practice the conversation. Listen and check your partner's pronunciation.

SPEAKING

A Walk around the class. Introduce yourself to everybody.

A: Hello, my name's Sven. Nice to meet you.
B: Hi, I'm Ahmed. Good to meet you.

B Walk around the class again. Greet the people you know.

A: Hi, Maria. How's it going?
B: Good, thanks. How about you? What's new with you?
A: Not much. I've gotta go. See you later.

C Prepare a 'selfie' presentation. Follow the instructions.

- Write notes about what you want to say. Use the sentence beginnings below to help you.
- Include at least two useful phrases.
- Record your presentation.

Hi! My name's …	I work in …
I'm from … / I'm originally from …	I like …
I'm a …	I watch / listen to …

D SPEAK Work in groups. Compare your presentations. Which is the best one?

Greet people and give personal information, make introductions

➤ Turn to **page XXIV** to learn how to write information about yourself.

Unit 1 Review

VOCABULARY

A Complete the words for types of people.

1 someone who likes animals
a nimal l over

2 someone who likes spending time with others
p________ p________

3 someone who plays video games
g________

4 someone who is very interested in food
f________

5 a man who has two children
f________ o________ t________

6 someone who listens to music regularly
m________ f________

B Complete the *About me* section of Emma's social media page with the personality adjectives in the box. There is one adjective you do not need.

creative curious ~~hard-working~~ independent sensible sociable well-organized

Hi, I'm Emma and I'm a student nurse. I study and work a lot 1(hard-working) and I make lists so I know what I am doing and when 2(______________). I always think carefully before I make decisions 3(______________). I feel it is important to ask a lot of questions 4(______________) in my social life and at work. I have a good imagination and in my free time I like to write songs 5(______________). I also have a great group of friends and I love spending time with them 6(______________).

C Choose the correct prepositions to complete the sentences.

1 In my family, we are all responsible *for* / *on* / *with* doing the housework.

2 I'm not interested *in* / *about* / *to* people who talk about themselves all the time.

3 As a child, I was involved *in* / *with* / *at* a lot of after-school clubs and activities.

4 I'm happy *at* / *with* / *on* my job.

GRAMMAR

A Complete the questions with the correct form of *do*, *be* or *have*.

1 Do you ________ a pet?

2 ________ you from a large family?

3 ________ you have a party for your last birthday?

4 ________ you ever been to your country's capital city?

5 What ________ your favorite book or toy when you were a child?

B Complete the article with the missing words.

Student Life Online
Your college, your site

This week, we asked students what blogs they read. This is what they said.

Erica: Most 1______________ the time, I read blogs about soccer.

Jake: 2______________ so often, I read a cooking blog.

Ammar: I 3______________ ever read blogs. I don't have time.

Mark: Once a 4______________, on Sunday mornings, I sit down and read my favorite travel blog.

Tina: 5______________ and then, I read news blogs.

Nazreen: I don't read blogs, but I do use Twitter. I check it at least ten 6______________ a day.

What are your favorite blogs? Leave your comments below.

C Choose the word which is *not* possible in each sentence.

1 *Everybody* / *Somebody* / *Anybody* can have nice handwriting.

2 I don't agree with *everything* / *anything* / *nothing* that the graphologists say.

3 Everyone *use* / *uses* / *has* a keyboard these days.

4 Do you know *anybody* / *anyone* / *anything* that is sociable?

FUNCTIONAL LANGUAGE

Reorder the words in the boxes to complete the conversations.

name's / Hi, / my / Erwin
myself / me / Let / introduce
meet / Nice / to / you

Erwin: 1 Hi, my name's Erwin.

Laura: Oh, hi, Erwin. 2______________________________. I'm Laura, the office manager.

Erwin: 3______________________________. I think you're going to be my boss!

nice / What / surprise / a
days / are / doing / What / you / these

Alan: Dan?

Dan: Alan! 4______________________________! How are you?

Alan: Oh, fine, thanks. 5______________________________?

Dan: I'm still teaching.

2 LIVING

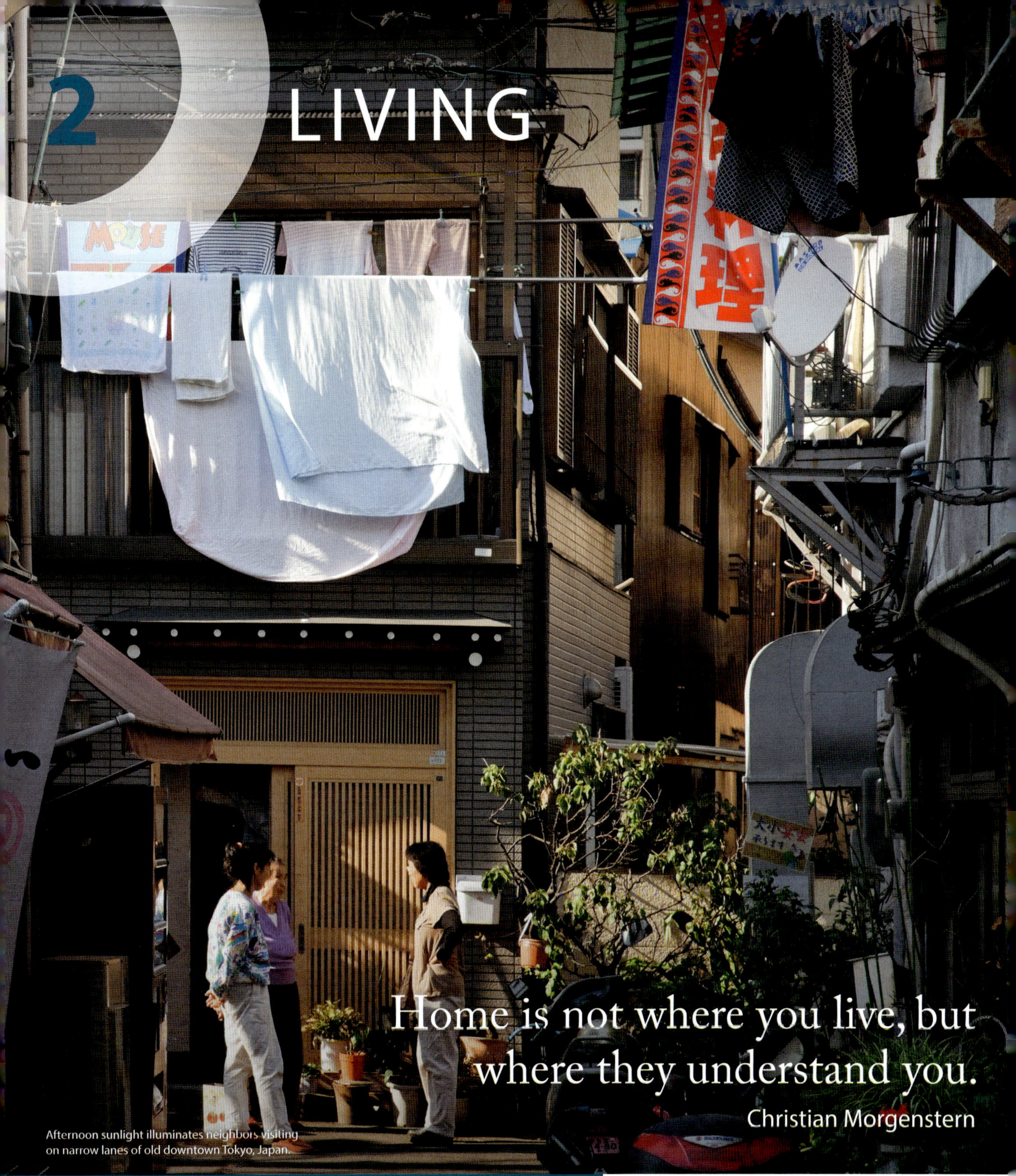

Afternoon sunlight illuminates neighbors visiting on narrow lanes of old downtown Tokyo, Japan.

> Home is not where you live, but where they understand you.
>
> Christian Morgenstern

OBJECTIVES

- talk about your neighborhood
- talk about your life and routine
- talk about life events
- ask for and give advice
- write an email of complaint

Work with a partner. Discuss the questions.

1 Read the quote. Where is 'home' for you?

2 Look at the picture. What do you think the people are talking about?

3 Do you know your neighbors?

2.1 Love where you live

Talk about your neighborhood

G adverbs of degree **V** describing places **P** stress in two-syllable adjectives

READING

A Work in pairs. Discuss the questions.

1. Do you love where you live? Why/Why not?
2. Look at the pictures. What can you see?
3. Look at the glossary. How can a building be environmentally friendly?

B SCAN Read *The forest in the sky* quickly and complete the sentences with the correct word or number from the text.

1. Bosco Verticale is an Italian name that means 'vertical ________.'
2. The apartment buildings are in the city of ________ in Italy.
3. There are almost ________ trees on the balconies of the buildings.
4. The plants help make the noise from the ________ and people in the street quieter.
5. The apartment buildings are close to the city's services and ________.
6. The architects plan to build another forest city in ________ in the future.

C READ FOR DETAIL Read again and answer the questions.

1. What are the four problems of life in central Milan that the writer mentions?
2. How do the Bosco Verticale buildings solve these problems?
3. What is the main problem with buildings like Bosco Verticale?
4. Does the writer think forest cities are a good idea?

D SPEAK Work in pairs. Answer the questions.

1. Do you want to see forest cities in your country? Why/Why not?
   Forest cities are a good idea because …
2. Should we pay more to live in clean cities? Why/Why not?
   I don't think we should pay more to live in clean cities because …

THE FOREST IN THE SKY

Where in the world can you live on the top floor of a 111-meter high-rise building, near the center of a **lively** city, but still have breakfast under a tree on your balcony? Sounds almost impossible! Well, not if you live in the Bosco Verticale (vertical forest) buildings in Milan, Italy. Architect Stefano Boeri has created a completely new approach to designing buildings.

Like many big cities, Milan is **noisy** and **polluted**. It's hot in the summer and in the city center the green spaces are usually fairly **crowded**. But Boeri's team have found a very green answer to these problems.

Almost 900 trees grow high above Milan on the balconies of **modern** buildings. The trees keep the apartments cool in summer and warm in winter. They also produce oxygen, which keeps the air **clean**. The buildings are so **quiet** because the trees and plants stop the noise from the people and traffic in the streets below.

Bosco Verticale is really **convenient** for the city's stores, services and transportation, it's **attractive**, and it's environmentally friendly. So, will there be more buildings like this in the future? Well, possibly. The architects want to build a new forest city in China and the Netherlands, but there is one more problem to solve. Buildings like this are extremely expensive. At 65 million euros, Bosco Verticale cost 5 percent more to build than a normal high-rise building. But if we want to live in cool, quiet cities with clean air, it will be worth the cost.

Glossary

architect (n) someone whose job is to design buildings
environmentally friendly (adj) something designed not to harm the natural environment
vertical (adj) standing, pointing or moving straight up

GRAMMAR

Adverbs of degree

A **WORK IT OUT** Complete the sentences from *The forest in the sky* with the correct adverbs of degree.

1 Sounds ________________ impossible!

2 Stefano Boeri has created a ________________ new approach to designing buildings.

3 Boeri's team have found a ________________ green answer to these problems.

B Underline four more adverbs of degree in the article.

C Choose the correct words to complete the rules.

> **Adverbs of degree**
>
> 1 Adverbs of degree are usually used *before* / *after* the adjective that they modify.
>
> 2 We *use* / *don't use* adverbs of degree when we want to make something stronger or weaker.
>
> 3 We *can* / *can't* use adverbs of degree with adverbs and verbs:
>
> - *She is speaking very fast.*
> - *He almost finished the race.*

D Go to the **Grammar Hub** on **page VIII**.

E **SPEAK** Work in pairs. Look at the pictures of unusual buildings and use adverbs of degree to describe them.

A: It's so different from a normal building.

B: It's very strange!

VOCABULARY

Describing places

A Read the sentences and look at the adjectives in **bold**. Then write the opposite adjectives.

1 The air in my city is fairly **clean**. There aren't many factories. ____dirty____

2 My neighbors are very **loud**. They usually play music late at night. ________________

3 It's a very **inconvenient** place to live. Our house is far from the stores and public transportation. ________________

4 The shopping center is very **old-fashioned**. It looks like it's from the 1970s. ________________

5 My apartment is in an **ugly** high-rise building. I don't like living there. ________________

6 The main streets are very **dirty**. People regularly drop trash. ________________

7 My neighborhood is very **peaceful**. I rarely hear cars or people in the street. ________________

B Use the adjectives in Exercise A to write five sentences about your neighborhood.

C **SPEAK** Work in pairs. Say an adjective. Your partner says the opposite. Take turns.

PRONUNCIATION

Stress in two-syllable adjectives

2.1 **A** Listen and underline the stressed syllable in each adjective.

1 dirty	3 modern	5 noisy
2 quiet	4 peaceful	

2.1 **B** Listen again and repeat the words.

C Most two-syllable adjectives have the same stress pattern. Read the text below and underline the stressed syllable in all the two-syllable adjectives.

> The Chang (Elephant) Building is in Bangkok, Thailand. Some people think it is modern and interesting; some people think it is strange and funny. Other people think it is ugly and totally awful!

SPEAKING

A Tell your partner about your neighborhood. Use these ideas to help you.

- Location – is it convenient? Close to public transportation?
- Appearance – is the area clean, modern?
- People – who lives there? Families or young professionals?
- Environmentally friendly – are there local parks?

B Work in pairs. Take turns to ask and answer your questions.

Talk about your neighborhood

2.2 The boomerang generation

● Talk about your life and routine

V verb + preposition G simple present and present progressive P consonant pairs at the beginning of words

LISTENING

A Work in pairs. Discuss the questions.

1 Why do people move out of their parents' home?
2 When do people usually leave home in your country?
3 Why do some adults continue to live at home?
4 What problems could this cause?

2.2 **B LISTEN FOR GIST** Listen to the first part of *The boomerang generation* and answer the questions.

1 What does 'boomerang generation' mean?
2 How old is Richard?
3 Why is Richard living at home with his parents?
4 Does he enjoy living at home?

Glossary

boomerang (n) a curved stick that comes back to you when you throw it
generation (n) a group of people in society who are born and live around the same time
permanent (adj) happening or existing for a long time

2.3 **C** Listen to all of *The boomerang generation* and match two questions with each speaker. Write Richard (R), Gordon (G), Alice (A) or Carla (C).

Who …

1 says their child can live at home for a long time? C
2 seems worried about their child? ___
3 isn't working right now? ___
4 plans to do something to thank their parents? ___
5 wants to make a change to their house? ___
6 likes living with their parents? ___
7 is happy they are not alone? ___
8 isn't happy with the house rules? ___

D SPEAK Work in pairs. What are the advantages and disadvantages of living with your parents as an adult?

VOCABULARY

Verb + preposition

2.4 **A** Complete the sentences from the radio show with the correct preposition. Then listen and check your answers.

1 I'm still looking ___ a permanent job.
2 We argue ___ the rules.
3 He can always rely ___ us.
4 I help ___ the housework.
5 I can talk ___ her.

Verb + preposition

Some verbs can be used with different prepositions to mean different things.

argue + about + something

- *We usually argue* ***about*** *housework.*

argue + with + someone

- *I usually argue* ***with*** *my parents.*

It is possible to join the sentences together:

- *I usually argue* ***with*** *my parents* ***about*** *housework.*

B Complete the email to Stella with the prepositions from Exercise A.

Re: Help?!
Sent: Friday, November 10, 2017, 2:19 pm
To: stella_28@logbox.com
From: d.smith@screen.nett

Hi Stella,

Thanks for calling this morning. Sorry to hear you're having money problems, but we're happy you decided to talk [1] to us about it. You can always rely [2] ___ us. I know you don't like borrowing money, but we'd like to help [3] ___ your rent this month. Let's not argue [4] ___ it this time. You can pay us back when you have a little more money.

You said you'd like to look [5] ___ somewhere cheaper to live. How about coming back to live [6] ___ us for a while? It would only be a temporary solution, but we'd like you to think [7] ___ it. Give us a call and let's talk [8] ___ it.

Lots of love,

Mom and Dad

C SPEAK Work in pairs. What should Stella do? Move home or find somewhere else to live?

A: I think she should definitely …
B: I'm not sure she should …

GRAMMAR

Simple present and present progressive

A WORK IT OUT Read the sentences from *The boomerang generation*. Are they simple present (SP) or present progressive (PP)?

1 I love my parents. ____
2 I'm sleeping in my old room. ____
3 Mom cooks and does all my laundry. ____
4 More and more of my friends are moving back home. ____

B Complete the rules with *simple* or *progressive*.

Simple present and present progressive

1 We use the ____________ present to talk about routines (events that happen every day) and things which are always or generally true.
2 We use the present ____________ to describe what is happening now and to talk about trends.
3 We do not usually use the present ____________ with state verbs like *be, like, want, understand, believe, know, mean, need, cost.*
4 We usually use the present ____________ with time expressions like *now, today, this year.*

C Go to the **Grammar Hub** on **page VIII**.

D SPEAK Work in pairs. Complete the sentences with information about your country and discuss with your partner.

1 Recently, more people are living *in apartments in the big cities*.
2 People love ____________, but they don't like ____________.
3 Everyone's talking about ____________ right now.
4 Many young people are studying ____________ ____________ right now.
5 Some people are happy because ____________ ____________.

PRONUNCIATION

Consonant pairs at the beginning of words

2.5 **A** Listen to the words and add them to the correct consonant group.

sl	sm	sn	sp	st	sw
sleep					

B SPEAK Work in pairs. Practice saying these words. Can you add one more example to each group?

SPEAKING

A You are going to ask your partner about his/her life and routine. Use the prompts to make simple present or present progressive questions.

1 think about / moving back home again?
Are you thinking about moving back home again?
2 save money / for anything this year?
____
3 like / cooking for yourself?
____
4 know / your neighbors?
____
5 your own question
____

B Work in pairs. Take turns to ask and answer your questions.

A: Are you thinking of moving back home?
B: I'm not sure. I need to save some money, so maybe!

Talk about your life and routine

2.3 Time flies

Talk about life events

G simple past – regular and irregular verbs
P Simple past irregular verbs /ɔː/, /e/ and /eɪ/
V life events
S skimming for key words

READING

A Work in pairs. Read the sentence from the article and discuss the questions.

When I was young, … a year was such a long time. Now I'm an adult, time passes so quickly.

1 Do you agree with this sentence? Why/Why not?
2 Can you think of an example when time passed quickly or slowly for you?

B READ FOR MAIN IDEA Read *When did the years get shorter?* quickly and match the headings (a–e) with each theory in the text (1–4). There is one heading you do not need. Use the information in the box to help you.

Skimming for key words

When you read an article for the first time, look for clues to help you understand the main idea of each paragraph.

- Look for key words. These could be numbers or the same words repeated.
- Look for words connected to the main topic.
- Look at the first sentence of each paragraph to help you understand the topic.

a The race against time
b From spring to winter
c New experiences slow down time
d It's all about the numbers
e Counting the days

C READ FOR DETAIL Read again. Are the sentences true (T) or false (F)? Correct the false sentences.

1 Time moved more quickly when the writer was a child. T / F
2 As we grow old, every year becomes a smaller percentage of our life. T / F
3 Many adults feel they have too much free time. T / F
4 Time slows down if we are looking forward to an event. T / F
5 New experiences can help to slow down time. T / F
6 All the theories agree that adults and children experience time differently. T / F

D SPEAK Work in pairs. Which theories in the article best explain why time seems to fly as we get older? Why? Give examples from your own life.

A: I like the one about …
B: I think Theory 3 is best because …

When did the years get shorter?

By Stefan Nyberg January 10, 2019

Glossary

routine (n) your usual way of doing things
stressful (adj) involving or causing a lot of pressure or worry
theory (n) an idea that explains how or why something happens

When I was young, the school summer vacation was six weeks long – it felt like forever. A year was such a long time! Now I'm an adult, time passes so quickly. Why does time seem to fly as we get older? Psychologists have several theories about this. Here are the most popular ones:

Theory 1: __

The first theory is mathematical. When you were 5 years old, a year was 20 percent of your life, so it seemed like a long time. When you are 50 years old, a year is only 2 percent of your life, so it seems much shorter. Time can feel very different if you are a child or an adult.

Theory 2: __

As children, we didn't have as much to worry about – we started school and studied, then we came home and played with our friends. Adult life is fast, busy and stressful – it's difficult to do everything we want to do. Days can be tiring. Many of us feel that there isn't enough time in the day. Time seems to pass very quickly because as adults we tend to rush to do something and then move on to the next job with no time to stop and think.

Theory 3: __

As children we knew exactly how many days it was until our next birthday or holiday. All that counting and waiting made the days seem to pass much more slowly. Some psychologists suggest adults don't notice time passing because they are focused on 'boring adult stuff', like shopping or housework. The days, weeks and months pass quickly. Suddenly, another year is over and a new one is beginning.

Theory 4: __

The routines of work and family life mean that, for many adults, the days all feel the same. This is different from our early lives, which were full of exciting first-time experiences. Back then, we started school and studied new things. Then we took exams, went on our first dates and learned to drive. When we look back on all these first-time experiences, we feel that the years were much longer because so many new things happened.

All these theories have something in common: there is a clear difference between the way adults and children experience time. Perhaps we need to learn from children and slow down a little more. Stop, look around, notice the blossom on the trees in the spring and the leaves changing color in the fall. The earth will keep spinning, but we are only here for a short time. Let's enjoy it!

GRAMMAR

Simple past – regular and irregular verbs

A **WORK IT OUT** Complete the sentences (1–4) from *When did the years get shorter?* Then match them with the correct simple past forms in the box below.

1 As children we _________ school and studied.

2 We _______________ exactly how many days it was until our next birthday or holiday.

3 As children, we _______________ have as much to worry about.

4 When _______________ the years get shorter?

negative regular question irregular

B Choose the correct options to complete the rules.

Simple past regular and irregular verbs

Simple past positive

1 To talk about ***finished*** / ***unfinished*** actions in the past.

2 For most regular verbs in the simple past tense, we add ***-ed*** / ***-ing***.

Simple past negative

3 We make the simple past ***negative*** / ***positive*** with subject + *didn't* + base form

Simple past questions

4 We ***make*** / ***don't make*** questions with *Did* + subject + base form + ?

5 Question words (*What*, *Where*, *When*, *Why* and *How*) come ***before*** / ***after*** *did*.

6 After *yes/no* questions, we use *did/didn't* in ***short*** / ***long*** answers.

C Go to the **Grammar Hub** on **page VIII**.

PRONUNCIATION

Simple past irregular verbs /ɔː/, /e/ and /eɪ/

2.6 **A** Complete the table with the words in the box. Listen and check.

~~ate~~ ~~bought~~ fought made paid ~~said~~ sent taught

/ɔː/	*bought*
/e/	*said*
/eɪ/	*ate*

B **SPEAK** Make questions about your childhood using the prompts. Ask and answer them with a partner.

1 Where / meet / your best friend?

2 What / your parents / teach you?

3 You / a happy teenager?

4 Your idea.

VOCABULARY

Life events

A Look at *When did the years get shorter?* again. Find four important life events and match them with the pictures (a–d). How old were you when you did these things?

B Go to **the Vocabulary Hub** on **page XVIII**.

C **SPEAK** Work in pairs. At what age do people generally do these things in your country? At what age did your grandparents' generation do these things? Tell your partner.

- learn to swim
- get married
- have a baby
- retire

SPEAKING HUB

A Work in groups. You are going to tell your group about three first-time experiences. Two should be true and one should be false. Use the ideas in the box or your own ideas.

first vacation without your parents
first child first important exams first job
first romantic relationship getting your own place
learning to ride a bike or drive leaving home
starting school or college

B **ORGANIZE** Answer the questions. Write notes.

- Where and when did you have this first-time experience?
- Who else was part of the experience?
- What happened? What went well? Were there any problems?
- How did you feel? Did you learn anything from the experience?

C **DISCUSS** Tell the group about your first-time experiences. Take turns. Can you guess which experiences are true and which are false?

Talk about life events

Café Hub

2.4 Noisy neighbors

F – ask for and give advice   P – disagreeing

COMPREHENSION

A SPEAK Work in pairs. Describe your neighbors to your partner. What are they like? Use words in the box to help you or your own ideas.

friendly   noisy   old   quiet   unfriendly   young

B Look at the picture. Why do you think Neena, Gaby and Zac are going to see their neighbor like this? Write notes.

Neena's problem	The advice	The decision

C ▶ 00:00–03:40 Watch the first part of the video and check your ideas in Exercise B. What do you think the neighbor is like?

D ▶ 03:40–04:04 Watch the second part of the video. Why does everybody laugh?

FUNCTIONAL LANGUAGE

Ask for and give advice

A Complete the sentences with the correct verb forms. Then decide who said each sentence, Gaby (G), Neena (N) or Zac (Z).

1 What do you think I should ***do / to do***? ___

2 You could ***ask / to ask*** them to turn the volume down. ___

3 How about ***to use / using*** some earplugs? ___

4 Let me ***help / to help*** you out here. Earplugs. ___

5 What ***do / are*** you suggest? ___

6 Why don't you ***go / to go*** upstairs and talk to them? ___

7 I think you should ***go / to go*** and talk to them. ___

8 And why don't we ***come / coming*** with you? ___

B ▶ Watch the video again and check your answers to Exercise A. Write the sentences in the correct place.

Ask for advice
What should I do?
1 ________________
2 ________________
Give advice
You should/shouldn't …
3 ________________
4 ________________
5 ________________
6 ________________
7 ________________
8 ________________
Reply
That's a good idea.
Thanks, I'll try them.
I'm not sure it's a good idea.

MILLY

SAM

NEENA

ZAC

GABY

C Complete the job interview advice for Neena with one word in each blank. Which do you think is the best piece of advice?

1 You ____________ leave plenty of time to get there.
2 I ____________ you should read about the company before the interview.
3 Here's one idea: you ____________ practice a few typical interview questions with a friend.
4 Nervous? ____________ don't you do some breathing exercises to relax?
5 I think you ____________ dress for success.
6 You ____________ have your phone on during the interview.
7 I ____________ think you should ask about salary first.

USEFUL PHRASES

A ▶ Match the useful phrases (1–6) with the phrases that come after them in the video (a–f). Then watch the video again and check your answers.

1 Seriously?!
2 What's wrong?
3 Cool!
4 Here you go.
5 What's the problem?
6 You can rely on us.

a No, it's not cool.
b All of us.
c Cool, thanks, Gaby.
d Someone's playing dance music in the flat above my bedroom.
e *(very loud dance music playing)*
f Oh Zac, the people upstairs are playing loud music.

B How do you say these useful phrases in your language?

PRONUNCIATION

Disagreeing

A ▶ 00:38–00:49 Watch the scene where Neena disagrees with Gaby again. Read out the conversation at the same time as Gaby and Neena. Copy the word stress and intonation.

Gaby: Really? Cool!
Neena: No, It's not cool. I need to get to sleep.

B **SPEAK** Work in pairs. Make similar conversations. Take turns to comment, disagree and say why. Use the comments in the box or your own ideas.

That's cheap/expensive! That's fair/unfair! That's funny/serious! That's good/bad! That's lucky/unlucky!

A: That's cheap!
B: No, it's not cheap. It's really expensive.

SPEAKING

A Work in pairs. Choose one of the problems and write a conversation with one friend giving advice to another one.

1 I usually forget my house keys.
2 My neighbor's dog barks all day.
3 The children in the apartment upstairs are very noisy.
4 My roommate spends too much time in the bathroom.
5 I'm the only person who does the cleaning.
6 My roommate's always hot and I'm always cold.

B Practice your conversation. Take turns giving advice. Then perform it for the rest of the class.

A: I usually forget my house keys.
B: Why don't you leave a key with your neighbor?
A: That's a good idea.

Ask for and give advice

➤ Turn to **page XXV** to learn how to write an email of complaint.

Unit 2 Review

VOCABULARY

A Complete the ad with the correct prepositions.

Samaritans is a UK charity that helps 1 ___with___ personal problems. Every six seconds, someone calls looking 2 ______ support. Callers can talk 3 ______ volunteers 24 hours a day and can rely 4 ______ them to listen and help. Many callers don't want to talk 5 ______ their problems with people they know well or live 6 ______. Samaritans volunteers keep all conversations private and are always there to help.

www.samaritans.org

B Complete the profile with the simple past forms of the verbs in the box.

change fall get go to have ~~leave~~

David Attenborough

1926 – born in London

1945 – 1 ___left___ school and 2 ______ Cambridge University

1946 – met and 3 ______ in love with Jane Ebsworth Oriel

1950 – 4 ______ married to Jane; the couple later 5 ______ two children, Robert and Susan

1952 – joined the BBC

1965 – became the head of television channel BBC Two

1973 – 6 ______ jobs and became the writer and presenter we know and love today

GRAMMAR

A Choose the best adverb of degree to complete the sentences. Use the information in parentheses to help you.

1 The idea of a vertical forest building sounds ***fairly*** / ***really*** interesting. (*STRONG*)
2 It's ***almost*** / ***totally*** impossible to add trees to every high-rise building. (*WEAK*)
3 The builders worked ***extremely*** / ***a little*** quickly. (*STRONG*)
4 The problem with buildings like this is they can be ***very*** / ***fairly*** expensive. (*WEAK*)
5 The trees are ***almost*** / ***so*** healthy because of rainwater. (*STRONG*)

B Complete the paragraph with the simple past or present progressive form of the verbs in parentheses.

Dreaming of Tokyo

Friends Tatsuo and Daisuki shared a small apartment in Tokyo for three years. Tatsuo 1 ___speaks___ (*speak*) French and recently left for a temporary job in Paris. He 2 ______ (*work*) there as a tour guide for the summer. Apartments 3 ______ (*cost*) a lot in Tokyo and Daisuki can't afford to stay. Right now, he 4 ______ (*live*) with his parents outside the city. They get along well, but Daisuki 5 ______ (*not like*) the two-hour daily train trip into Tokyo.
He is not the only one in this situation. More of his friends 6 ______ (*leave*) the city these days because it's so expensive. Every morning, the train Daisuki 7 ______ (*catch*) is full of young people, making the long trip to work and dreaming of their own place in the city.

C There is one mistake with the simple past in each sentence. Correct the mistake.

1 I ~~falled~~ *fell* in love when I was 18.
2 I weren't good at sports when I was a teenager.
3 I didn't thought money was important when I was a child.
4 When I was young, my parents always knowed when I wasn't telling the truth.
5 I leaved home when I was 19.
6 My father teached me how to drive.
7 I wasn't meet my partner at work.

FUNCTIONAL LANGUAGE

A Complete the missing words in the conversation.

Sophie: Peter, I can't stand the course I'm studying in college. 1W *h a t* d__ you t__ __ __ __ I s__ __ __ __ __ do?
Peter: 2M__ __ __ you s__ __ __ __ __ wait and see if things improve.
Sophie: 3I s__ __ __ __ __ __ s__, but I'm pretty sure the course is not for me.
Peter: 4W__ __ d__'__ y__ __ talk to your teacher about it?
Sophie: 5T__ __ __'__ a good i__ __ __.
Peter: 6D__ you w__ __ __ m__ t__ go with you?
Sophie: No, that's OK, but thanks.

3 TRAVEL

To travel is to live.
Hans Christian Andersen

Canoeing through the early morning mist near Port Angeles, Washington, US.

OBJECTIVES

- talk about journeys and transportation
- tell a story about a journey
- talk about the kind of vacations you like
- ask for travel information and check understanding
- write an email about a travel experience

Work with a partner. Discuss the questions.

1 What can people learn from traveling?
2 Look at the picture. Do you enjoy doing outdoor activities?
3 Where is the last place you traveled to?

3.1 The four-year journey

● Talk about journeys and transportation

G *all / some / most / no / none* **V** types of transportation **P** /p/, /b/, /v/

British man Graham Hughes is the first person to visit all of the countries in the world without flying.

Hughes traveled by sea and over land to complete his record-breaking journey. He traveled on a budget of only US $150 a week and paid for everything himself. Thirty-three-year-old Hughes set off on New Year's Day 2009. His first stop was Argentina, and 1,492 days later, he arrived at his final destination, South Sudan. Hughes crossed the borders of all of the 193 United Nations countries. He traveled long distances by boat, and for shorter trips went by train, rode a bus or occasionally took a taxi. None of his trips were by plane. A lot of people helped him on his journey. Some of them gave him directions and food or let him sleep on their couch for free, and others gave him rides.

Of course, not all his experiences were good. He also had some problems. He crossed the Sahara Desert, but had to go back 2,000 miles because he didn't have the correct visa. The most difficult place to get to was the Seychelles. Graham tried three times from three different countries before he finally made it to the islands.

Glossary

budget (n) the amount of money a person has to spend on something
visa (n) an official document that allows you to enter or leave a country for a specific time period

READING

A Work in groups. Think of a country beginning with each letter of the alphabet. You have two minutes.

B SCAN Work in pairs. Read the first line of the article about Graham Hughes. What might the information in the box refer to? Read the article and check your answers.

150 US dollars | 193 countries | 1,426 days | 2,000 miles

C SPEAK Work in pairs. Would you like to do a similar journey to Graham? Why/Why not?

D READ FOR DETAIL Read again. Are the sentences true (T) or false (F)? Correct the false sentences.

1 The United Nations helped Graham pay for his journey. *T / F*
2 His journey finished in Argentina. *T / F*
3 People were kind to Graham during his journey. *T / F*
4 He didn't always pay for accommodations. *T / F*
5 He visited the Seychelles three times. *T / F*
6 He went on his journey because he wanted to help people from all over the world. *T / F*

E SPEAK Work in pairs. Discuss the questions.

1 Would you let a stranger sleep on your couch? Why/Why not?
2 Graham says the world is full of people who want to help each other. Do you agree? Explain your answer.

GRAMMAR

all / some / most / no / none

A WORK IT OUT Look at these sentences from the article about Graham Hughes. Then choose the correct words to complete the rules.

Hughes crossed the borders of ***all of*** *the 193 United Nations countries.*

None of *his trips were by plane.*

Some of *them gave him directions and food …*

Of course, not ***all*** *his experiences were good.*

He also had ***some*** *problems.*

all / some / most / no / none

1 We use *all, some, most, no* **before / after** nouns.
2 We **can / can't** use *all, some, most, none* with *of* + pronoun.
3 We **can / can't** use *all, some, most, none* with *of* + *the / this / that / these / those*.
4 We **can / can't** use *no* with *of* + pronoun or *the / this / that / these / those*.
5 With *all* we **have to / don't have to** use *of* before a pronoun or *the / this / that / these / those*.

B Go to the **Grammar Hub** on **page X**.

C SPEAK Work in pairs. Make sentences of your own with *all / some / most / no / none*. Talk about:

- my friends
- my travel experiences
- types of transportation
- Graham Hughes or people like him

VOCABULARY
Types of transportation

A Find five types of transportation in the article about Graham Hughes. Write them in the correct place. Then add the words in the box.

car ferry helicopter minibus trolley

Travel by air	Travel over land	Travel by ocean
plane		

Transportation collocations

With all the transportation nouns in Exercise A, we can use the verbs *go* or *travel* + *by*. We don't use *a* / *an* before the noun. We can also use *take* or *get* + *a* / *an*.

- *He traveled long distances by boat, and for shorter trips went by train, rode a bus or occasionally took a taxi.*

When we talk about plane travel, we usually use the verb *fly*.

- *We flew to Portugal last summer.*

B Add (+) or remove (–) one word to make each sentence correct. Use the Transportation collocations box in Exercise A to help you.

1 I go to work by a bus everyday. (–)
2 My brother occasionally gives a ride on the back of his motorcycle. (+)
3 I took taxi home last Saturday night. (+)
4 I usually get by a trolley to my English classes. (–)

PRONUNCIATION
/p/, /b/, /v/

3.1 **A** Listen and repeat.

1 /p/ plane 2 /b/ boat 3 /v/ visa

3.2 **B** Listen and write the words in the correct place.

/p/	/b/	/v/
	bus	

3.3 **C** Listen, check and repeat the words.

SPEAKING

A Interview your classmates about their travel habits. Find out about:

- daily travel to and from college or work
- trips they regularly make on the weekend
- transportation they use to go on vacation

B Work in pairs. Write questions to find out about:

- the different types of transportation people use in each type of travel in Exercise A
- what they like and dislike about each type of transportation they use
- how much they spend on transportation in a normal week

C Interview another student and make a note of their answers to your questions.

D Work with your original partner again and compare the travel and transportation habits of the people you interviewed.

1 Who uses more types of transportation?
2 Who feels most positive about the transportation they use?
3 Who spends the most on transportation in a normal week?

Talk about journeys and transportation

3.2 Lost at sea

Tell a story about a journey

G past progressive and simple past **P** *was* and *were* with past progressive **V** prefixes

LISTENING

A What famous stories or movies do you know that involve seas, oceans and islands? What happens?

B PREDICT Work in pairs. You are going to listen to a podcast about the Robertson family. Look at the pictures (1–4). What do you think happened?

3.4 **C** Listen and check your answers to Exercise B.

Glossary

brave (adj) a brave decision, action or choice is one that you make even though it involves risk and may cause problems for you
life raft (n) a small rubber boat used for saving people whose boat is sinking
survival expert (n) a person who knows how to stay alive in emergencies if you are far away from help
survive (v) to stay alive, especially in a difficult or dangerous situation, for example injury, illness, war

3.4 **D LISTEN FOR DETAIL** Listen again and put the information in the order that you hear it (1–6).

___ The Robertsons got help.
_1_ One of the Robertsons' children asked an unusual question.
___ The Robertsons had no more food.
___ The Robertsons left their old life behind.
___ There was a serious accident.
___ The Robertsons made it back to land.

E SPEAK Work in pairs. Discuss the questions.

1 Do you think the Robertsons' decision to sail around the world was a good one? Why/Why not?
2 Why do you think some people do dangerous things?
3 Do you ever do dangerous things, or do you prefer to avoid danger? Give examples.

GRAMMAR

Past progressive and simple past

A WORK IT OUT Read the rules and complete the examples with the words in the box.

bought noticed sold started was passing were living

Past progressive and simple past

We use the past progressive (*was / were* + verb + *-ing*) for actions or situations that were in progress.

- *In 1970, Dougal and Lyn Robertson and their four children* 1 ________ *on a farm, in northern England.*

We use the simple past for finished actions or situations, and things that happened one after another.

- *They* 2 ________ *their business,* 3 ________ *a boat and on January 27th, 1971,* 4 ________ *their journey across the Atlantic.*

When used together in the same sentence, the past progressive describes a long action and the simple past describes a shorter action.

- *Their boat* 5 ________ *the Galapagos Islands when they* 6 ________ *something large in the water behind them.*

when* and *while

We use **when** or **while** to link past progressive and simple past verbs.

We can use **when** or **while** before the past progressive.

- ***When/While*** *they were sailing out into the Pacific Ocean, things started to go very wrong.*

We always use **when** before the simple past.

- *They were sailing out into the Pacific Ocean* **when** *things started to go wrong.*

AMAZING ADVENTURES

1

2

B Go to the **Grammar Hub** on **page X**.

C **SPEAK** Think of an interesting or unusual thing that happened to you on a trip or vacation. Write notes using the questions below. Then work in groups and tell your story.

1 Where and when was the vacation?

2 Who did you go with?

3 What happened that was interesting or unusual?

4 What were you doing when this thing happened?

When I was a teenager, I went camping with my family in Spain. One morning, we were walking to the beach when I found a wallet full of money on the path ...

PRONUNCIATION

was and *were* with past progressive

3.5 **A** Listen and repeat the sentences. What do you notice about *was* and *were*?

1 We were biking to the beach when I fell off my bike.

2 I was swimming in the ocean when I lost my car keys.

B **WORK IT OUT** Choose the correct words to complete the rules.

1 We usually use ***weak*** / ***strong*** pronunciation of *was* and *were* in positive sentences.

2 We do this because we ***stress*** / ***don't stress*** the main verb.

C **SPEAK** Work in pairs. Find out what your partner was doing at these times.

1 7 am this morning

2 last New Year's Eve at midnight

3 10 pm last night

VOCABULARY

Prefixes

A Look at the sentences from *Amazing Adventures*. Choose the correct words to complete the rules.

I mean, they were very ***un****lucky, weren't they, Matt?*

It sounds like an ***im****possible situation.*

1 We use prefixes before ***adjectives*** / ***pronouns*** to change their meanings.

2 Prefixes like *un-*, *im-*, *dis-* and *in-* give the original word a(n) ***opposite*** / ***stronger*** meaning.

B Complete the words with the correct prefix, *un-*, *im-*, *dis-* or *in-*.

1 I don't believe anything he says. I think he's ____**honest**.

2 Living on rainwater and turtles sounds very ____**healthy** to me.

3 I failed the test; a lot of my answers were ____**correct**.

4 Not many people go to the Galapagos Islands. It's a/an ____**usual** vacation destination.

5 He doesn't like waiting – he's very ____**patient**.

C **SPEAK** Work in pairs. Think of other examples of things or people that you can describe with the adjectives with prefixes in Exercises A and B.

SPEAKING

A Work in groups and describe a journey. Students A and B – go to the **Communication Hub** on **page XXIII**. Students C and D – go to the **Communication Hub** on **page XXIII**.

B Work in pairs. Take turns telling your story to your group.

C Work in groups. Look at all eight pictures as a group and think of a new story that uses them all. Then tell your story to another group.

3

4

Tell a story about a journey

3.3 Too good to be true

● Talk about the kind of vacations you like

G verb + *-ing* and *to* + base form **V** accommodations and amenities **P** /ʃ/, /tʃ/ and /dʒ/ **S** identifying tone

READING

A Work in pairs. Discuss the questions.

1 When you are planning a vacation, how do you choose where to stay?

2 Do you find online reviews helpful or not? Why?

B Read two online reviews for a hotel. Which sounds real and which does not? Why?

★★★★☆

a I love to travel, but I can't afford to stay in five-star hotels or expensive apartments all the time. If you are on a budget like me, the three-star Hotel Jasmine is a great choice. The service is very good and the rooms are small but clean. The location is a little noisy but central. I hope to return to Hotel Jasmine soon.

★★★★★

b This hotel is EXCELLENT!!! The rooms are BEAUTIFUL and the staff are very kind and WONDERFUL!!! I love shopping and the hotel is in the city center!!! I will definitely go on using this hotel – in fact, I refuse to stay anywhere else!!!!!

C **SCAN** Read *Tips for a happy vacation* quickly. Underline any of the ideas you discussed in Exercise B.

D Choose two words which describe the author's tone. Use the information in the box to help you.

1 serious
2 informal
3 formal
4 funny

Identifying tone

The tone of a text can help you understand the author's opinion on the topic. Notice words and phrases the author uses to communicate this.

- Look at the author's choice of adjectives and adverbs.
- Does the punctuation give you any clues? For example, 'quotation marks', exclamation marks, parentheses or capital letters.
- Is the language formal or informal?

TIPS FOR A HAPPY VACATION

You're **planning** to go on vacation and you've **decided** to try somewhere new. You could **consider** using a travel agent, but it's easy to organize your own vacation online these days. All you **need** to do is visit a travel review site, spend time reading travelers' comments and then choose the accommodations with the best reviews. Simple!

Or is it? How do you know that what you are reading is genuine? Research shows that some hotels and restaurants pay people to write fake reviews. Of course, the websites **manage** to find and delete some of these fake reviews, but they aren't always successful. So, before you **choose** to spend your vacation budget on that 'amazing beach resort' or cruise ship that scored ten out of ten, read our tips and learn how to spot a fake review.

TIP ONE: What you see is not always what you get. If the pictures of the apartment, guest house or campsite **seem** to be too good to be true, they probably are. For example, when you see the photograph below, you **expect** to find a nice quiet beach, but in fact, the beach and all the hotels are right next to a building site!

TIP TWO: Nowhere is perfect – fact! Most genuine reviewers **like** to include a mix of positive and negative comments, so a review that's 100 percent positive or negative is more likely to be fake. If you **want** to know what a hostel or chalet is really like, don't read the very best and very worst reviews. Look at the ones in the middle.

TIP THREE: EXCELLENT!!!!!!!! Fake reviewers **like** using capital letters, exclamation marks (!) and lots of extreme adjectives like 'wonderful', 'amazing' and 'excellent'. It can feel like you are being YELLED AT! Genuine reviewers usually **avoid** using so much extreme language. Instead, they usually include helpful details like room size or prices.

Glossary

fake (adj) made to look like something real in order to trick people

genuine (adj) real, rather than pretended or false

E READ FOR DETAIL Read again and answer the questions.

1 Why isn't organizing your own vacation online as simple as it seems?
2 Why might someone want to write a fake review?
3 What does the article aim to teach its readers?
4 What are the characteristics of a genuine review?
5 What are the characteristics of a fake review?

F SPEAK Work in groups. Discuss the questions.

1 What other kinds of online reviews do you read or write, for example, movies, books, games, etc.?
2 Do people rely too much on online reviews? Explain.

GRAMMAR

verb + *-ing* and *to* + base form

A WORK IT OUT Look at the underlined verb patterns from the online reviews. Then complete the rules with the words in the box.

either   *to* + base form   verb + *-ing*

1 I love to travel, but I can't afford to stay in five-star hotels or expensive apartments all the time.
2 I hope to return to Hotel Jasmine soon.
3 I love shopping and the hotel is in the city center!!!
4 I will definitely go on using this hotel – in fact, I refuse to stay anywhere else!!!!!

verb + *-ing* and *to* + base form

1 We use ________ after these verbs: *agree, can't afford, hope, learn, refuse, would like, would prefer,* ________, ________, ________, ________, ________, ________

2 We use ________ after these verbs: *(don't) mind, enjoy,* ________, ________.

3 We can use ________ after these verbs (there is little change in meaning): *hate, love, prefer, (can't) stand,* ________.

B Look at *Tips for a happy vacation* again. Write the verbs in **bold** in the correct place in Exercise A.

C Go to the **Grammar Hub** on **page X**.

D SPEAK Work in pairs. Think about the best place you have stayed on vacation. Write a short review. Then swap with a partner and ask questions about your partner's review.

VOCABULARY

Accommodations and amenities

A Look at the words in the box. Which types of accommodations are included in *Tips for a happy vacation?*

apartment   beach resort   campsite   chalet
cruise ship   guest house   hostel   hotel

B Go to the **Vocabulary Hub** on **page XIX**.

C SPEAK Work in groups. Take turns describing or drawing items from the **Vocabulary Hub**. The first person in the group to guess each item gets one point.

A: This keeps your room cool when the weather is hot.
B: Air conditioner!

PRONUNCIATION

/ʃ/, /tʃ/ and /dʒ/

3.6 **A** Listen to the sounds. Are they the same or different? Then listen and repeat.

1 /ʃ/ chalet   2 /tʃ/ choose   3 /dʒ/ budget

3.7 **B** Complete the table with the words in the box. Listen, check and repeat.

~~adjective~~   ~~beach~~   genuine   language
manage   picture   ~~ship~~   shout   show

/ʃ/	/tʃ/	/dʒ/
ship	*beach*	*adjective*

C SPEAK Work in pairs. Practice saying the words. Listen and check your partner's pronunciation.

SPEAKING HUB

A Work in groups. You are going on vacation together to Barcelona for two nights. Together, you have a budget of 600 dollars for accommodations and spending money. Answer the questions:

1 What kind of accommodations would you like to stay in?
2 Which amenities are most important to your group?

B Read about vacation accommodations in Barcelona.
Student A – go to the **Communication Hub** on **page XXII** and read about Hotel Rambla Park.
Student B – go to the **Communication Hub** on **page XXII** and read about Gaudí House Hostel.
Student C – go to the **Communication Hub** on **page XXII** and read about Olympic Apartments.

C PRESENT Describe the accommodations you read about to your group. Decide where you will stay. How much spending money will you have left?

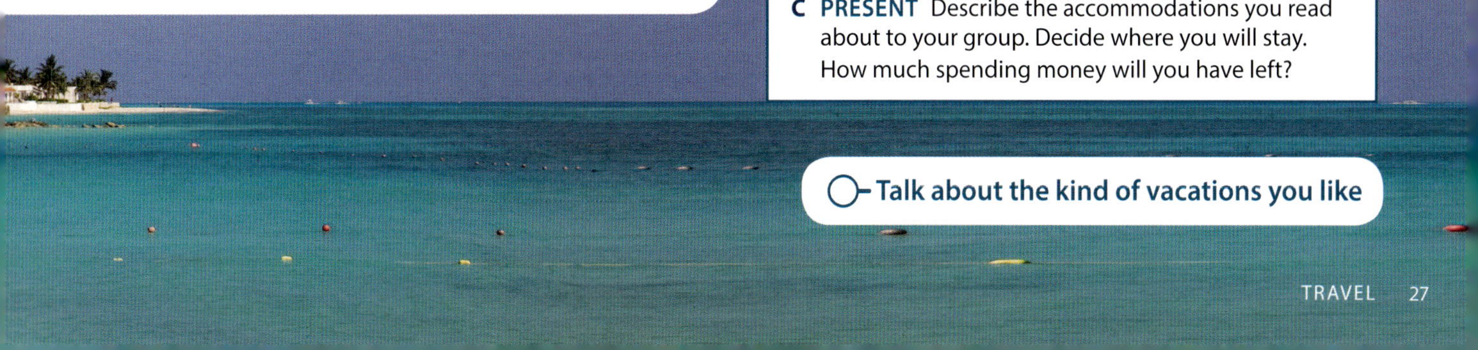

Talk about the kind of vacations you like

3.4 Overslept

F– ask for travel information and check understanding
P– word stress and intonation

COMPREHENSION

A SPEAK Work in pairs. Are you usually early or late for things? Give examples.

B SPEAK Work in pairs. Number the pictures in order (1–6) to describe a morning when Gaby overslept. What do you think happened?

a ☐

b ☐

c ☐

d ☐

e ☐

f ☐

C ▶ Watch the video and compare it with your ideas in Exercise B. What does the ticket officer find? What do you think will happen next?

FUNCTIONAL LANGUAGE

Ask for travel information and check understanding

A Test your memory! Look at the conversation between a customer and a ticket officer. Underline five responses that are different from the video. Try to remember the correct information.

Ask for travel information – trains	
Customer:	[1]Could I have a ticket to St. Albans?
Ticket officer:	[2]Of course. Would you like a single or a return?
Customer:	[3]A single, please.
Ticket officer:	[4]No problem.
Customer:	[5]Do I have to change trains?
Ticket officer:	[6]Yes, you need to change at Watford.
Customer:	[7]What time's the next train?
Ticket officer:	[8]The next train's in about ten minutes. [9]The next train leaves from platform 4B.
Customer:	[10]What time does the train arrive in St. Albans?
Ticket officer:	[11]At 9:13.

B ▶ Watch the video again and check your answers to Exercise A. Write the correct information.

Glossary

single **(adj) (British)** = one-way **(adj) (American)**
return **(adj) (British)** = round-trip **(adj) (American)**

MILLY SAM NEENA ZAC GABY

USEFUL PHRASES

A Watch the video without sound. Yell *Stop!* when you think the ticket officer is about to use one of the useful phrases. Then listen and check.

1 Here, let me help you.
2 Don't worry.
3 Follow me.
4 Don't forget this.
5 You don't want to miss your train.
6 Have a good trip.

B How do you say these useful phrases in your language?

PRONUNCIATION

Word stress and intonation

3.8 **A** Listen and repeat the conversation. Copy the word stress and intonation.

Ticket officer: The next train's in about three minutes from platform two.
Anna: I'm sorry. Did you say three minutes?
Ticket officer: Yes, three minutes!
Anna: OK, thanks. Oh, and where's platform two?
Ticket officer: Go past the coffee shop, then turn right.
Anna: OK. So I need to go past the coffee shop and then … turn left? Is that right?
Ticket officer: No, you need to turn right after the coffee shop.

B SPEAK Work in pairs. Make a similar conversation.

SPEAKING

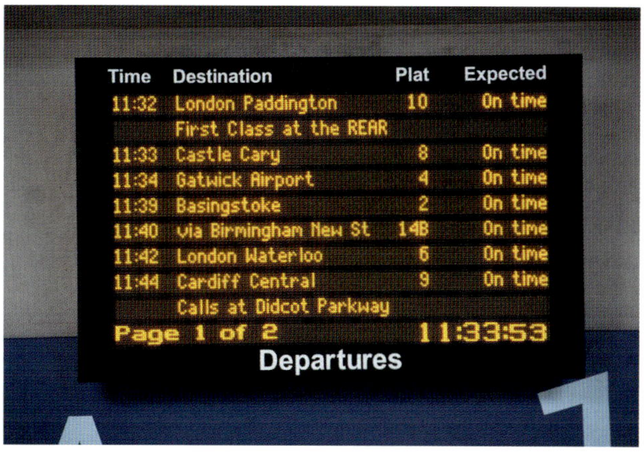

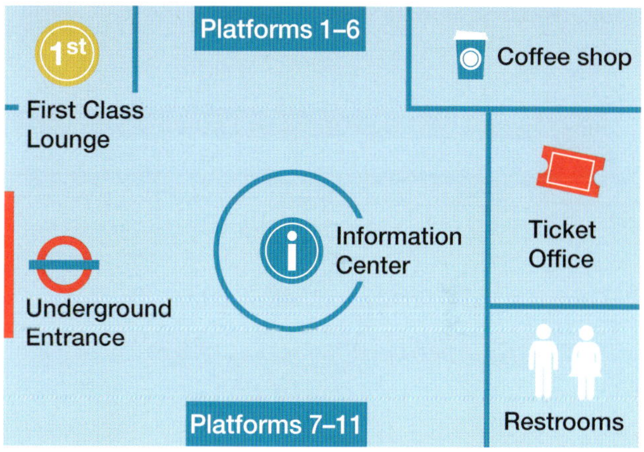

A Work in pairs. Student A is the customer. Student B is the ticket officer. Write a conversation. Use these ideas to help you.

Student A: Ask for information about trains to a place on the departure board.
Student B: Answer Student A's questions.
Student A: Check understanding and then ask for directions to the correct platform.
Student B: Look at the train station plan and give directions.
Student A: Check understanding.

B Practice your conversation. Take turns being the customer and the ticket officer. Then perform it for the rest of the class.

Ask for travel information and check understanding

➤ Turn to **page XXVI** to learn how to write an email about a travel experience.

Unit 3 Review

VOCABULARY

A Label the pictures with the correct forms of transportation.

bus ferry helicopter minibus plane trolley

1 ______________

2 ______________

3 ______________

4 ______________

5 ______________

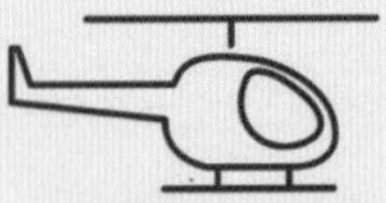

6 ______________

B Write the words in the box in the correct place. Some words can go in more than one place.

accurate happy kind likely organized polite

un-	im-	dis-	in-

C Complete the definitions with the words in the box.

apartment beach resort campsite chalet cruise ship

1 A ______________ is a place where people on vacation can stay in tents.

2 A ______________ is a large, comfortable boat that has similar amenities to a hotel.

3 A ______________ is a place that many people go to for a vacation by the ocean.

4 A ______________ is a wooden house built in a mountain area where people on vacation can stay.

5 An ______________ is a set of rooms, usually on one floor of a large building, where people on vacation can stay and cook their own meals.

GRAMMAR

A Choose the correct words to complete the sentences.

1 *Most* / *Most of* the people I know want to visit other countries.

2 *Some* / *Some of* countries are difficult to get into.

3 *No* / *None* type of transportation is completely safe.

4 *All the* / *All* my money was in my jacket.

B Complete the article with the past progressive or simple past forms of the verbs in parentheses.

Lucky to be alive!

Today, we bring you the story of surfer Mick Fanning.

World champion surfer Mick Fanning is lucky to be alive. In 2015, he [1]______________ (*surf*) in a competition in South Africa when a shark [2]______________ (*attack*) him. Thousands of people [3]______________ (*watch*) on live television when the attack [4]______________ (*happen*). Mick [5]______________ (*sit*) on his surf board when he [6]______________ (*notice*) the shark next to him. The giant fish tried to pull him under the water, but Mick [7]______________ (*hit*) it on the back, and it [8]______________ (*swim*) away. A rescue boat [9]______________ (*wait*) and it brought Mick and another surfer safely back to land.

C Choose the correct form of the verbs to complete the questions. Both forms may be possible.

1 Do you ever refuse ***to leave*** / ***leaving*** a tip in a restaurant? Why?

2 Do you prefer ***to go*** / ***going*** on vacation in the summer or the winter? Why?

3 What do you hope ***to learn*** / ***learning*** when you visit a new country?

4 Would you enjoy ***to visit*** / ***visiting*** a country where no one speaks your language? Why/Why not?

5 Do you like ***to try*** / ***trying*** new foods when you travel? Give an example.

FUNCTIONAL LANGUAGE

A Write the words in the correct order to make questions.

1 have / a / could / I / ticket / to / Central Station / ?

____

2 a / one-way / you / like / would / a / round-trip / or / ?

____

3 does / train / what / the / arrive / in / time / Amsterdam / ?

____

4 next / the / time's / train / what / ?

____

5 do / trains / have / I / to / change / ?

____

6 did / say / platform / sorry, / I'm / 30 / you / ?

____

7 is that right / at the top of the stairs, / so it's left / ?

____

8 do / get / you / to / platform / 9 / how / excuse me, / ?

____

B Work in pairs. Think of different ways to answer the questions in Exercise A.

4 SOCIALIZING

> Man is by nature a social animal.
>
> Aristotle

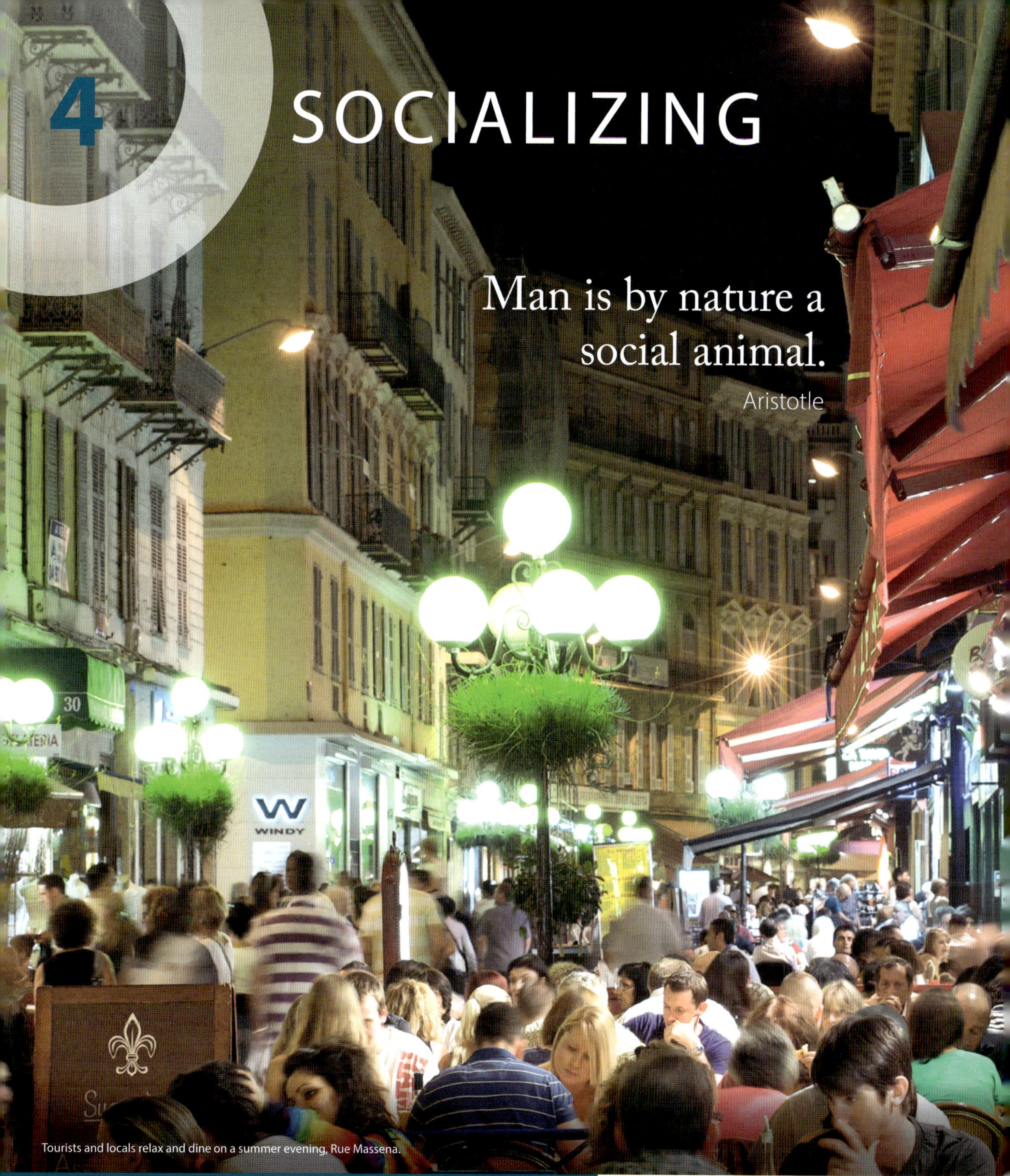

Tourists and locals relax and dine on a summer evening, Rue Massena.

OBJECTIVES

- **talk about plans you have made for a weekend with visitors**
- **present reasons to support or argue against predictions**
- **ask and answer questions about how you like to spend your free time**
- **make arrangements to meet up with somebody**
- **write an invitation and reply**

Work with a partner. Discuss the questions.

1. Where do people go out in your country?
2. Look at the picture. Which city do you think it is? Why?
3. What do you enjoy doing with your friends?

4.1 What's the plan?

Talk about plans you have made for a weekend with visitors

V free time **G** *be going to* + base form and present progressive for the future **P** *going to*

VOCABULARY

Free time

A SPEAK Work in pairs. Write down as many free time activities as you can in English. You have two minutes. Then compare your list with another pair.

B Complete the diagrams with the verbs in the box.

go for | go to | hang out | play | see or go to

1 ____________ : the theater / the movies; a museum / a gallery; a market; a friend's place / a party

2 ____________ : a meal / a drink; sushi/pizza/burgers; a walk / a run / a bike ride; coffee/lunch/dinner

3 ____________ : an exhibit; a concert / a play / a movie; a comedy show

4 ____________ : cards; board games; pool/billiards

5 ____________ : in town; at the mall; online; in the park; with friends

C SPEAK Work in pairs. Which of the free time activities in Exercise B are your favorites, and why?

LISTENING

A Work in pairs. What kind of things do you like to do when you visit a city for the first time?

4.1 **B LISTEN FOR GIST** Listen to a conversation between Sylvia and Greg and circle seven free-time activities in Vocabulary Exercise B that they talk about.

Glossary

arrange (v) to make plans for something to happen, for example by agreeing on a time and place

intelligent (adj) good at understanding difficult ideas and subjects

4.1 **C LISTEN FOR DETAIL** Listen again and choose the correct answer a or b.

1 What is the relationship between Sylvia and Greg?
   a brother and sister
   b boyfriend and girlfriend

2 Who is Claire?
   a Greg's friend
   b Greg's girlfriend

3 Sylvia thinks that Greg will like her friend Duncan because they …
   a are both good cooks.
   b both enjoy eating.

4 After dinner, Sylvia and Greg are going to see …
   a a comedy show.
   b a play by Shakespeare.

5 Greg stops Sylvia explaining the plan for the next day because he …
   a doesn't feel very well.
   b wants to order some food.

D SPEAK Work in pairs. When was the last time you visited friends or family for the weekend? Tell your partner.

GRAMMAR

be going to + base form and present progressive for the future

A **WORK IT OUT** Read the definitions. Then look at the sentences and decide if they are arrangements (A) or intentions (I).

Arrangements – you have probably booked a ticket or agreed on a time with other people. You usually mention a time, date or place.

Intentions – you have already decided to do something and want to tell someone about it. You don't need to mention a time, date or place.

1 I'm going to introduce you to all my new friends as 'Greggy'. ___
2 Tomorrow evening, she's having dinner with some old friends. ___
3 I think I'm going to bring Mom and Dad here, too. ___
4 We're meeting Duncan and Alicia at three o'clock. ___
5 Alicia says she and Duncan are going to open a restaurant one day. ___

B Choose the correct words to complete the rules. Use Exercise A to help you.

***be going to* + base form and present progressive for the future**

1 We use *be going to* + base form to talk about ***arrangements / intentions***.
2 We use the present progressive (*be* + verb + *-ing*) to talk about ***arrangements / intentions***.

C Go to the **Grammar Hub** on **page XII**.

PRONUNCIATION

going to

4.2 **A** Listen and repeat the pronunciation of *going to* /ˈgʌnə/ in informal speech.

1 She's going to call later.
2 I'm going to text Angie and Mark.

B **SPEAK** Work in pairs. Look at the sentences that you marked as intentions (I) in Grammar Exercise A. Practice saying the sentences in an informal way. Pronounce *going to* as /ˈgʌnə/.

C **SPEAK** Ask questions about your partner's plans. Talk about your arrangements and intentions.

A: Are you going to have a party in the next few weeks?
B: Yes, I am! It's my birthday next weekend and I'm having a party.

SPEAKING

A Work in groups. Plan a weekend. Choose a group of visitors:

- older family members, for example, an aunt and uncle or grandparents
- younger family members, for example, a brother or sister with their partner and children
- a group of four friends from school or college

B Make plans for next weekend for you and your visitors in and around a city you know well. Write notes on:

- meeting
- sightseeing
- entertainment
- food and drink
- evening activities

C Explain your plan to students from other groups. Which weekend sounds like the most fun?

My old school friends are coming to visit next weekend. I'm meeting them at the train station. Then we're going to have breakfast in town, probably at Vincent Café. The food there is great and it isn't expensive.

Talk about plans you have made for a weekend with visitors

4.2 The future of free time

Present reasons to support or argue against predictions

G making predictions P *will* and *won't* V suffixes

READING

A Work in pairs. Do you agree with the following sentences? Why/Why not?

In the next ten years …

we will do less work and spend more time socializing.

we will do a lot of our socializing in virtual worlds.

we will socialize with artificial intelligence.

B **READ FOR MAIN IDEA** Work in groups. Student A go to **page XXIII**, Student B go to **page XXII** and Student C go to **page XXIII**. Read your article and discuss the questions below.

1 What does the article say about our social lives?
2 What role will technology play?
3 Which expert or business leader is mentioned, and why?
4 What possible benefits of the development does the article mention?

C **SPEAK** Work in groups. Discuss your article and the following questions.

1 Which predictions do you think will happen?
2 Do you think these will be positive or negative developments for our social lives? Why?

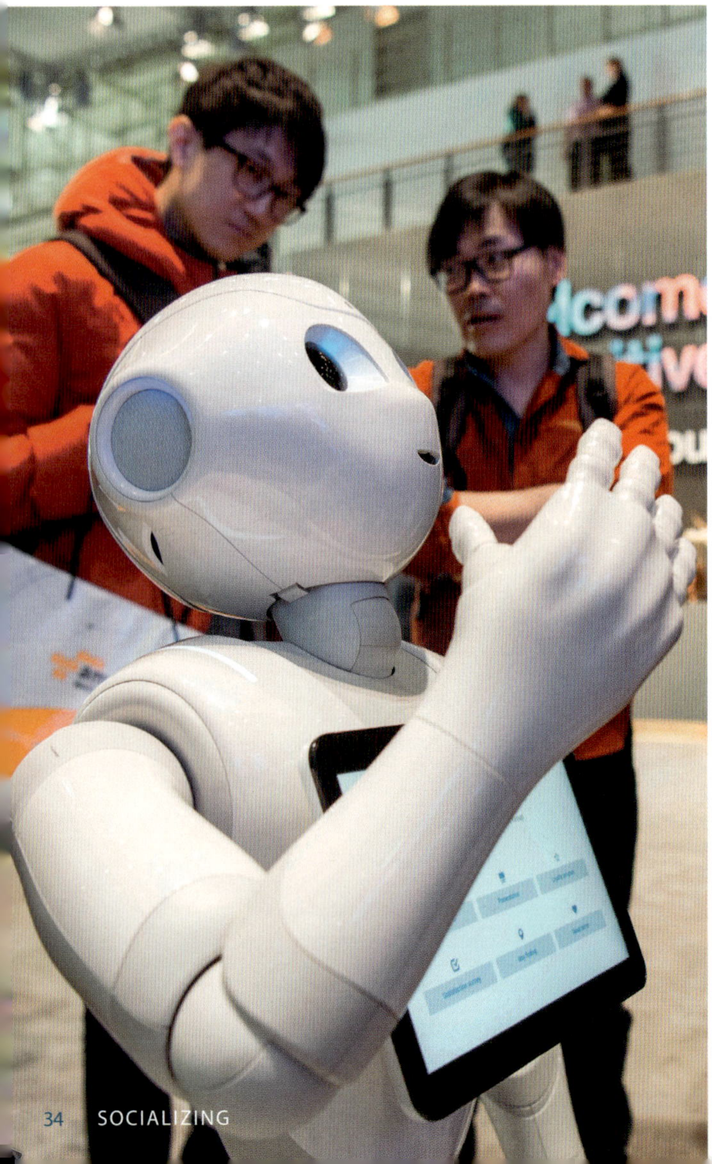

GRAMMAR

Making predictions

A **WORK IT OUT** Look at the sentences from the articles about the future of our social lives. Underline the modal verbs used to make predictions.

1 The good news is some people think it might not be long until every weekend is a long weekend.
2 However, experts agree that the way we use social media will change in the future.
3 Some experts even believe that one day it may be possible for robots to feel love.

B Find and underline four more examples of modal verbs in one of the articles you read in Reading Exercise B. Then work in pairs and compare your answers.

C Complete the rules with *will* or *might/may*.

Making predictions

1 We use ______________ (*not*) + the base form of a verb when we are certain about our prediction.
2 We use ______________ (*not*) + the base form of a verb when we are less certain about our prediction.

D Look at the sentences from *Robot relationships*. Then choose the correct words to complete the rules.

… humans will probably develop close relationships with robots.

… it definitely won't be long until robots look, sound and move like humans.

1 We use *probably* to make predictions with *will* and *won't* **less** / **more** certain.
2 We use *definitely* to make predictions with *will* and *won't* **less** / **more** certain.
3 We use *probably* and *definitely* **before** / **after** *will*.
4 We use *probably* and *definitely* **before** / **after** *won't*.

E Go to the **Grammar Hub** on **page XII**.

F Complete the predictions about artificial intelligence with the words in parentheses.

1 Some people might not want three-day weekends every week. (*might not*)
2 It probably be harder to find a job in the future because of technology. (*will*)
3 I don't think we have robot friends in my lifetime. (*'ll*)
4 We control computers with our minds in the future. (*might*)
5 VR headsets definitely get much cheaper in the next few years. (*will*)
6 Humans won't fall in love with robots in the future. (*probably*)
7 I'm sure we all have robots in our homes 20 years from now. (*'ll*)
8 We stop working completely one day because of technology. (*may*)

G SPEAK Work in pairs. Are there any predictions in Exercise F that you do not agree with?

I think most people will want three-day weekends every week.

PRONUNCIATION
will and *won't*

4.3 **A** Stressed words are the ones that carry the information. Listen and underline the stressed words.

1 There will be fewer car trips to work in the future.
2 Technology will do more of the work for us.
3 People won't be paid for working fewer days per week.
4 Do you think people will be happier in the future?
5 No, they won't.
6 Yes, they will. They won't have to work so hard.

4.3 **B** Listen again and repeat the sentences. Copy the stress.

VOCABULARY
Suffixes

A Go to the **Vocabulary Hub** on **page XX**.

B Add one of the suffixes in the box to the words in parentheses to make nouns. You may need to change the spelling of some of the words. You will need to use some of the suffixes more than once.

-ion -ity -ment -ness

1 I think there is a ____________ (*possible*) that robots will feel love in the future.
2 I agree with the ____________ (*predict*) that virtual reality will be an important part of social media.
3 There is an ____________ (*agree*) between many experts that technology will help our work–life balance.
4 An important ____________ (*develop*) is that robots are now beginning to understand our feelings.
5 I don't believe that robots will be able to experience real ____________ (*happy*) or ____________ (*sad*).

C SPEAK Work in pairs. Look at sentences 1, 2 and 5 in Exercise B. Do you agree with these opinions? Why/Why not?

SPEAKING

A Discuss some predictions about the future. Read three predictions for the future and present reasons to support and argue against each.

Fifty years from now …

1 cash in the form of bills and coins will completely disappear.
2 all cars will be self-driving and there will be very few road accidents.
3 all European children will learn Mandarin at school.

B Work in groups. Discuss the predictions and write down reasons to support and argue against each prediction.

C Work in new groups. Take turns speaking for one to two minutes about one of the predictions.

Present reasons to support or argue against predictions

4.3 Hygge

Ask and answer questions about how you like to spend your free time

G subject and object questions **V** relaxing **P** linking a consonant to a vowel **S** summarizing

READING

A Work in pairs. Which of these things have you done recently? What exactly did you do? Tell your partner.

1. spend the evening at a friend's home
2. relax at home on your own
3. invite people over to your home for the evening
4. get together with your extended family
5. have a night out with friends

B SPEAK Look at the pictures. What are the people doing? How do you think they feel? Use the words in the box to help you.

a cozy blanket	a family gathering	a fire	a hot bath
a sleeping pet	candles	warm socks	wool sweaters

C READ FOR MAIN IDEA The pictures all show the Danish idea of *hygge*. What do you think *hygge* means? Read the first paragraph of *Make yourself at home* to check your answer.

Make *yourself* at home

What is *hygge*?

Winters in Denmark are long, dark and cold, but according to the 2016 UN World Happiness Report, Danish people are among the happiest in the world. One reason might be *hygge*, the Danish attitude that focuses on enjoying the simple things in life, such as enjoying a coffee in a relaxed atmosphere with easy-going friends or family.

How do you pronounce *hygge*?

Hygge is easy enough to pronounce – 'hue-gah' – but much more difficult to translate. No single English word describes the idea completely, but being cozy is a big part of it. There may be a connection between the word *hygge* and the English word *hug*, and in Danish *hygge* can be an adjective, verb or noun.

How do I know if it's *hygge*?

Your friends come over on a cold winter evening to sit by the fire, eat homemade food and play board games. That's definitely *hygge*. You have a quiet night in, take a bath, light some candles, then sit down with a good book and a cozy blanket. That's *hygge*, too. You argue about politics, check your phone, play video games and listen to thumping techno music. That's definitely not *hygge*! So how do you know if it's *hygge*? Think warm socks, wool sweaters, sleeping pets and happy family gatherings. Got it now?

Why *hygge*?

Research shows that people who are kind to themselves and take some time out to relax have better mental health and feel happier. *Hygge* encourages us to do this and also to get together with friends and family. Happy groups of people make more caring communities and a happier society. It's no surprise that the Danes are always smiling!

Glossary

cozy (adj) warm and comfortable, and making you feel relaxed

family gathering (phrase) when a family meets and spends time together

translate (v) to change spoken or written words into another language

D READ FOR DETAIL Read the whole article. Then complete the summary with the words in the box. Use the information in the box to help you.

Summarizing

A summary gives the most important points of a text.

Highlight or underline key points and write notes as you read the text. Try to use your own words rather than copy the writer's.

comfortable explain health important technology

Hygge is a Danish custom for people who want to relax and feel [1] ______________. It is usually at home and no [2] ______________ is involved! *Hygge* can be with other people or by yourself – the [3] ______________ thing is to feel happy and cozy. Feeling this way is good for your mental [4] ______________. This might [5] ______________ why Danish people were described as some of the happiest people in the world by the 2016 UN World Happiness Report.

E SPEAK Work in pairs. Discuss the questions.

1 When did you last do something '*hygge*'? What was it and who were you with?

2 Is there a word in your language that means *hygge* or something similar?

GRAMMAR

Subject and object questions

A WORK IT OUT Read the rules and look at the questions from *Make yourself at home*. Then look at the examples and answer the questions (1–3).

Subject and object questions

We ask subject questions when we don't know *what/who/which/whose* something or someone is.

We ask object questions when we want to know more information about something or someone.

What is hygge?

How do you pronounce 'hygge'?

1 Which is the subject question?

2 Which is the object question?

3 Which question includes an auxiliary verb?

B Look at the questions and possible answers. Then choose the correct words to complete the rules.

What is hygge? It is an attitude that focuses on enjoying the simple things in life.

How do you pronounce 'hygge'? You pronounce it 'hue-gah'.

1 With subject questions, we *change* / *don't change* the word order in the answer.

2 In *subject* / *object* questions, the question word is the object of the sentence.

C Go to the **Grammar Hub** on **page XII**.

D Choose the best question word and decide if an auxiliary verb is needed to complete the questions. Then choose the correct question type: subject (S) or object (O).

1 Who / Why is do / – your best friend? S / O

2 When / What do / – you do with your best friend? S / O

3 What / Who does smile / smiles more, you or your best friend? S / O

4 What / Which do / – you do to relax? S / O

E SPEAK Work in pairs. Ask and answer the questions in Exercise D.

VOCABULARY

Relaxing

A Work in pairs. Make a list of different ways of relaxing. You have one minute.

B Go to the **Vocabulary Hub** on **page XX**.

PRONUNCIATION

Linking a consonant to a vowel

A SPEAK Work in pairs. Which letters of the alphabet are vowels and which are consonants?

4.4 **B** Listen and repeat the phrases. Which words link together?

1 light a candle

2 take a bath

4.5 **C** Say the phrases and draw an arrow where a consonant sound links to a vowel sound. Then listen and check your answers.

1 have some friends over

2 a relaxed atmosphere

3 the simple things in life

4 friends and family

SPEAKING HUB

A Work in pairs. You are going to write a quiz with the title *Are you a home bird or a party animal?*

B PLAN Ask five questions and give two or three possible answers for each. Use the topics below:

- a favorite way of celebrating
- a typical Saturday night
- your ideal vacation
- going to or having parties
- eating out or cooking at home

C Swap quizzes with another pair and answer their questions. Do you agree with the results?

Ask and answer questions about how you like to spend your free time

Café Hub

4.4 Would you?

F – make arrangements to meet up with somebody

P – saying *yes* or *no*

COMPREHENSION

A SPEAK Work in pairs. Look at the pictures and discuss where the characters are and what you think happens. Then choose the correct words to complete the sentences.

1. Zac and Milly *have* / *haven't* met before.
2. Zac *knows* / *doesn't know* what to say to Milly.
3. Zac *wants* / *doesn't want* to buy a T-shirt.
4. Milly *likes* / *doesn't like* Zac.
5. Zac *likes* / *doesn't like* Milly.
6. Zac and Milly *arrange* / *don't arrange* to go out together.

B ▶ Watch the video and check your answers to Exercise A.

C ▶ **02:58–04:19** Watch part of the video again. When are Milly and Zac free to meet? Put a check mark (✓) or an ✗ in the correct place.

	Milly	Zac
1 tonight		
2 on Saturday after 1:30		
3 on Sunday at midday		

D SPEAK Work in pairs. Why are they not able to meet tonight or on Saturday?

Glossary

midday **(n) (British)** = noon **(n) (American)**

FUNCTIONAL LANGUAGE

Make arrangements to meet up with somebody

A Complete the questions with the words in the box. There are three words you do not need.

are can could do how maybe what will ~~would~~ would

Make arrangements (invitations)

1. *Would* you like to hang out tonight?
2. ________ you like to do something, then?
3. We ________ go for a coffee, or eat something?
4. ________ you free on Saturday?
5. ________ about Sunday instead?
6. ________ time?
7. ________ you want to meet at the park?

Say *yes*

Yeah! Sure. / Sounds great. / Awesome!

I'd love to!

Great. Twelve o'clock it is!

Say *no*

I'm so sorry, I can't.

Oh! Wait a minute. I just remembered …

B ▶ Watch the video again and check your answers to Exercise A.

MILLY

SAM

NEENA

ZAC

GABY

USEFUL PHRASES

A Match the useful phrases (1–6) with the phrases which show the correct meaning (a–f).

1 Are you looking for anything in particular?
2 I'm sorry, I need to get that.
3 So, you were saying.
4 Well, it was nice to see you again.
5 Wait, hold on!
6 Sounds great!

a I'm leaving.
b That's a good idea.
c Stay here!
d Do you want to buy something?
e Please continue.
f The phone is ringing.

B How do you say these useful phrases in your language?

PRONUNCIATION

Saying *yes* or *no*

4.6 **A** Listen and write the replies in the correct place.

Saying *yes*	Saying *no*

4.7 **B** Listen and repeat. Can you hear the difference in intonation between saying *yes* and saying *no*? Copy the word stress and intonation.

C SPEAK Work in pairs. Practice saying the replies. Listen and check your partner's pronunciation.

SPEAKING

A Work in pairs. Look at some things you could arrange to do. One item in each word set is not correct. Cross it out and replace it with your own idea.

1 go for … a drink / a walk / a drive / a shop
2 go to … the movie theater / swim / a gig / the beach
3 go … shopping / eating / swimming / dancing / biking

B Work in pairs. Practice making arrangements using the ideas in Exercise A. Take turns inviting each other.

Student **A:** Invite B to do something.
Student **B:** Say *no*.
Student **A:** Suggest another time.
Student **B:** Say *no*.
Student **A:** Suggest *another* time.
Student **B:** Say *yes*.

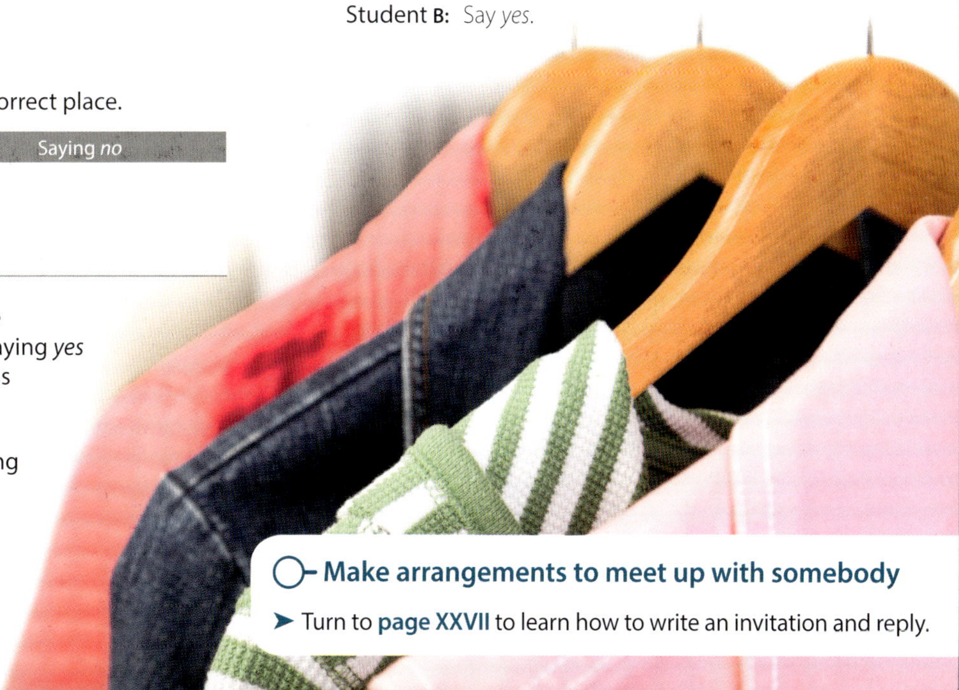

Make arrangements to meet up with somebody

➤ Turn to **page XXVII** to learn how to write an invitation and reply.

Unit 4 Review

VOCABULARY

A Write the missing words to complete Olivia's email.

To: Natalie
Subject: This weekend

Hi Natalie,

I have a great weekend planned for us. On Friday, I'll meet you at the station – then let's [1]________ for sushi and go [2]________ a drink in town.

On Saturday, we can go for a bike [3]________. I have two bikes, so let's take them and go [4]________ the market. After we can hang [5]________ in the park and talk or [6]________ cards.

On Saturday evening, we're going [7]________ my friend Alex's place. Then on Sunday, maybe we can [8]________ a movie before you go.

Can't wait!

Olivia xxx

B Choose the correct words to complete the sentences.

1 This robot can do a lot of different *active* / *activities*.
2 I think we should have a *discussion* / *discuss* about what will happen in the future.
3 What kind of *abilities* / *able* do you think machines will have in 50 years?
4 In my opinion, *happiness* / *happy* is one of the most important things in life.
5 There is the *possible* / *possibility* that people will stop using social media.

GRAMMAR

A Complete the sentences with *be going to* + infinitive or the present progressive form of the verbs in parentheses. Use contractions.

1 I ________________ (*not forget*) my friend's birthday again this year.
2 We ________________ (*meet*) the others tonight on the corner by the coffee shop.
3 Mia ________________ (*take*) her friend out for dinner tomorrow.
4 I think I ________________ (*lie down*) for a while before we go out.
5 Go to bed early because we ________________ (*get up*) at 6 am to drive to the airport.

B Find and correct the mistake in each sentence.

1 It will be easier to meet people in the future probably because of technology.
____
2 People might going on virtual dates online in the future.
____
3 A virtual date probably won't very romantic.
____
4 We might to use technology to help us choose the perfect partner.
____
5 The way people meet and fall in love not may change very much.
____

C Complete the questions and answers with the words in the box. You need to use some of the words more than once.

did	do	don't	it's	make
spend	went	what	which	

1 '*Which* country is *hygge* from, Denmark or Sweden?'
'________ from Denmark.'
2 'Who ________ you spend time with?' 'I ________ a lot of time with my best friend.'
3 '________ is your favorite book?' '________ *The Lord of the Rings*.'
4 'Which board games ________ you play?' 'I ________ play board games.'
5 'How ________ you celebrate your last birthday?'
'I ________ out for dinner.'

FUNCTIONAL LANGUAGE

Look at the beginning and end of the telephone conversation. Put the rest of the conversation in the correct order.

John: Dean, it's your brother. You OK?
Dean: Yep, fine thanks, and you?
__ John: That's great. There's just one thing … Jenny and I are going out.
__ Dean: Not really. No plans. Why?
__ John: Well, yes.
__ John: Well, we have an invitation to a new restaurant and …
__ Dean: And, you need a babysitter!
1 John: I'm great, thanks. Listen, are you doing anything this evening?
__ John: Do you want to come over? Jenny has made a curry dish and little Sam says he misses his Uncle Dean.
__ Dean: A curry dish and my favorite nephew? I'd love to!
__ Dean: What?
Dean: Fine, fine. What time?
John: You are the best. How about seven o'clock?

5 WORK

There is no substitute for hard work.

Thomas Edison

Electrical lineman Chen Qi cleans snow from a high-voltage transmission tower, Baima Mountain, Wulong County, China.

OBJECTIVES

- talk about the pros and cons of different jobs and say how they help society
- decide on the rules for a workplace or classroom
- answer questions on topics in which you are an expert
- give information about your work experience in a job interview
- write a cover email

Work with a partner. Discuss the questions.

1 What do you like about your job or the subjects you study?

2 Read the quote. What do you think Edison meant? Do you agree with him?

3 Look at the picture. Would you like to have this man's job? Why/Why not?

5.1 Work

- Talk about the pros and cons of different jobs and say how they help society

G – *can, could, be able to* **V** – work collocations **P** – /w/ and /v/

READING

A Match the definitions (1–4) with the words in the box.

pay raise salary self-employed well-paid

1 working for yourself ___________
2 a fixed amount of money that you earn each month or year from your job ___________
3 paid a lot of money ___________
4 an increase in the amount of money you are paid to do your job ___________

B SPEAK Work in pairs. What are four things, apart from money, that can make people happy at work?

C SCAN Read *What really makes us happy in our jobs?* quickly. Which of your ideas from Exercise B can you find?

D READ FOR DETAIL Read again. Who says these things make them happy in their job, Helen (H), Lena (L), Bret (B) or Ken (K)?

1 they have flexible vacations and working hours ___
2 they learn and use special skills ___
3 their employer gives them clear goals ___
4 they are independent ___
5 they have a relaxed manager ___
6 they have time for the family ___

E SPEAK Work in pairs. Which of the four jobs in the article would you rather have? Why?

What really makes us ***happy in our jobs?***

In a recent survey about jobs and work, 75 percent of children under ten said 'yes' to the question 'Can money buy happiness?' But is being **well-paid** really so important? Can you still be happy at work if you earn a **low hourly wage**? We asked four working adults what, apart from money, they like about their jobs.

Helen Police Officer

I don't work regular office hours – I do shifts. This means I often work in the evenings and sometimes do the night shift. In my last job I could choose when I wanted to work and I found that I liked working in the evenings. I also like that I am able to use all the different skills I learned when I was training to be a police officer.

Lena Sales Manager

I earn an average salary. However, if I make a lot of sales, I get a bonus and I find that motivating. I also enjoy having clear goals, even when I have to work long hours to achieve them. I recently got a promotion which meant a lot of extra work, but I don't mind. I got a small pay raise and as a manager I was able to take an extra afternoon off each week to spend with my kids.

Bret Waiter

My job is poorly paid, but I only work weekends, so I can study during the week. I work in a big restaurant. When there are no problems, the boss is usually very easygoing.

Ken Architect

The best part of my job is being my own boss. Because I'm self-employed, I can choose when I work and can take long vacations when I want to. The only bad part is I don't get a company car!

Glossary

bonus (n) extra money you are paid in addition to your usual salary, usually because you have done well, for example, *a year-end bonus*
promotion (n) a move to a higher level in your job, usually because you have done well

GRAMMAR

can, could, be able to

A WORK IT OUT Look at the sentences from *What really makes us happy in our jobs?* Then complete the rules with *can*, *could* or *be able to*.

I only work weekends, so I can study during the week.

I am able to use all the different skills I learned when I was training.

In my last job I could choose when I wanted to work.

I was able to take an extra afternoon off each week.

can, could and *be able to*

1 We use *can* and __________ to talk about possibility and ability in the present.

2 We use __________ and *was / were able to* to talk about possibility and ability in the past.

3 We usually use __________ or *was / were able to* for possibilities and abilities at a particular time or for a particular reason.

4 We use __________ immediately before the main verb because *can* has no *-ing* form or *to* + base form.

B Go to the **Grammar Hub** on **page XIV**.

C SPEAK Work in pairs. Discuss the questions.

1 What are some of your abilities?

2 What were some of your abilities as a child?

VOCABULARY

Work collocations

A Complete the questions with the correct form of the verbs in the box. Sometimes more than one answer is possible. You need to use some verbs more than once.

be earn get take work

1 Do you or anyone you know __________ shifts? How often do they do a night shift?

2 Do you know anyone who __________ a very high salary? What do they do?

3 Do you think people should __________ an automatic pay raise every year they stay in the same job?

4 Who __________ the longest hours out of all the people you know? What do they do?

5 When was the last time you __________ a day off? What did you do?

6 Would you prefer to __________ a company car or more money?

7 Do people who __________ unemployed get money from the government in your country?

8 Would you be motivated by a job where you earn an average salary, but have the chance to __________ a bonus? Why/Why not?

B SPEAK Work in pairs. Would you like to be your own boss? Why/Why not? Tell your partner.

PRONUNCIATION

/w/ and /v/

5.1 **A** Listen to the sounds. Are they the same or different? Listen and repeat.

1 /w/ work 2 /v/ very

5.2 **B** Listen and write the words in the correct place.

/w/	/v/
wage	*involve*

5.3 **C** Listen and check your answers. Then listen and repeat.

D SPEAK Work in pairs. Can you think of more words with the sounds /w/ and /v/? Make a list.

SPEAKING

A Work in groups. Go to the **Communication Hub** on **page XXII** and look at your group's list of jobs. Discuss the questions for each job.

1 Who do you know that does these jobs? How do they feel about them?

My brother is a social worker. He works with people that have serious problems, but he still enjoys it.

2 Is each job paid a high, medium or low wage or salary?

3 What are the best and worst parts of each job?

4 Give each job a category which describes how it helps society, for example, *important for entertainment, health, education*.

B Work in new groups. Tell the group about the jobs you discussed and the categories you chose in Exercise A. Discuss which categories of jobs are most valuable to society and why.

Talk about the pros and cons of different jobs and say how they help society

5.2 Flip-flop entrepreneurs

Decide on the rules for a workplace or classroom

G – obligation, necessity and permission: *must*, *have to* and *can* P – *can* / *can't* and *must* / *must not* V – adjectives for appearance

READING

A SPEAK Work in pairs. How important to you are the things on the list when you are buying new clothes? Decide whether they are very important (1), fairly important (2) or less important (3). Compare your ideas.

The product …

a is available in different colors and designs. ___

b is fashionable. ___

c is popular with celebrities. ___

The company …

a pays its staff fair wages. ___

b gives money to charity. ___

c does charity work. ___

B SCAN Read *How do you build a children's home out of flip-flops?* Which things in Exercise A are mentioned?

C READ FOR DETAIL Read again and answer the questions.

1 What was unusual about Rob and Paul's education?

2 How did the brothers become orphans?

3 Why did the brothers start Gandys?

4 Which six adjectives are used to describe the company's flip-flops?

5 What was unusual about the brothers' visit to Buckingham Palace?

D SPEAK Work in groups. Discuss the questions.

1 Who do the biggest charities help in your country? What do they do to help?

2 Do you give money to charity? Why/Why not?

How do you build a children's home out of flip-flops?

British brothers Rob and Paul Forkan have experienced tragedy and success in their short and unusual lives. When they were still children, their parents took them out of school in the UK and moved the family to India to travel and do charity work. The experience taught them about life in other places and made them confident and independent.

Tragedy struck in 2004 when the Asian tsunami hit the coast of Sri Lanka, where the Forkans were staying. The giant wave killed their parents, but Rob (17), Paul (15) and their younger brother and sister survived. The children, now orphans, managed to hitchhike across Sri Lanka to the airport. From there, they flew back to Britain, where friends and family were waiting.

Six years later and now adults, the brothers decided to do something in memory of their parents. Their idea was simple. Make and sell attractive casual footwear and use the profits to help other orphans. Their company *Gandys* and their charity *Orphans for Orphans* were born.

After a lot of hard work and with the support of celebrity customers such as Richard Branson and Jamie Oliver, the comfortable rubber flip-flops became a hit. Customers love *Gandys*' stylish and fashionable designs and that the brothers give ten percent of the profits to their charity. In 2014, three years after *Gandys* began, *Orphans for Orphans* opened its first children's home in Sri Lanka.

Gandys' head office now employs a large team and is possibly the only office in London where you can wear flip-flops to work! Rob and Paul's charity work has even gotten them an invitation to meet British princes William and Harry. Normally of course, you must wear dress clothes at Buckingham Palace, but the brothers ignored the dress code and looked cool in their colorful flip-flops!

Rob and Paul's story shows that positive can follow negative and that you don't have to wear a business suit to be successful in business!

Glossary

hitchhike (v) to have people give you a ride in their car, usually by standing on the side of the road and holding out your thumb or a sign

in memory of someone (phrase) in honor of someone who has died, so that people will remember them

tragedy (n) a very sad event that causes people to suffer or die

GRAMMAR

Obligation, necessity and permission: *must*, *have to* and *can*

A WORK IT OUT Look at the last two paragraphs of *How do you build a children's home out of flip-flops?* and complete the sentences.

1 You ______________ wear flip-flops to work.
2 You ______________ wear a business suit to be successful in business.
3 You ______________ wear dress clothes at Buckingham Palace.

B Match the modal verbs (1–4) with the meanings (a–d).

Obligation, necessity and permission: *must*, *have to* and *can*

1 *don't have to*
2 *must / have to*
3 *can*
4 *can't / must not*

a This is necessary or is a rule.
b This is not necessary but allowed.
c This is allowed but not necessary.
d This is not allowed.

C Choose the correct word to complete the rule.

Obligation, necessity and permission: *must*, *have to* and *can*

Modal verbs, such as *have to*, *can* and *must* are followed by the ***base form / simple present form*** of a verb.

D Go to the **Grammar Hub** on **page XIV**.

PRONUNCIATION

can / can't and *must / must not*

5.4 **A** Listen to the pairs of sentences. Can you hear the differences?

1 a You can wear casual clothes.
  b You can't wear casual clothes.
2 a Staff must not wear sportswear.
  b Staff must wear sportswear.

5.5 **B** Listen and check (✓) the sentence you hear.

1 a You must wear large earrings. ☐
  b You must not wear large earrings. ☐
2 a You can wear a baseball cap. ☐
  b You can't wear a baseball cap. ☐
3 a You must leave your coat downstairs. ☐
  b You must not leave your coat downstairs. ☐
4 a You can hang your coat on your chair. ☐
  b You can't hang your coat on your chair. ☐

VOCABULARY

Adjectives for appearance

A SPEAK Work in pairs. Make a list of adjectives to describe appearance. You have one minute.

cool, casual ...

B Match the adjectives (1–7) with the definitions (a–g).

1 attractive
2 casual
3 colorful
4 cool
5 fashionable
6 well-dressed
7 stylish

a show good judgement about how to dress well
b relaxed and comfortable
c pleasant to look at
d impressive and modern
e clean and neat
f popular at a particular time
g has bright or many different colors

C Choose the words that you agree with most. Then work in pairs and explain why.

1 I ***do / don't*** think it's important to wear dress clothes to work.
2 I think that flip-flops are ***too casual / perfect*** for wearing around town.
3 I prefer clothes with ***colorful / cool and simple*** designs.
4 I think it ***is / isn't*** important to wear fashionable clothes.
5 You ***can / can't*** be stylish without wearing expensive clothes.
6 People ***spend too much / don't spend enough*** time and money trying to look attractive.

SPEAKING

A Work in groups. Think about the place where you work or study. Answer the questions.

1 What are the most important rules?
2 What annoying or unnecessary rules are there?
3 What rules would you add to make it a better place to work or study?

B Work in groups. Write ten rules for the perfect workplace or classroom. Think about what is/isn't allowed and what is/isn't necessary. Use these ideas:

Workplace: rules for workers, managers and directors; working hours; pay; dress code, etc.

Classroom: rules for students and teachers; during classes; homework; tests and exams, etc.

C Look at the rules written by other groups. Which are the most useful? Why? Are there any you do not agree with? Why?

Decide on the rules for a workplace or classroom

5.3 Don't call us

● Answer questions on topics in which you are an expert

G present perfect with *for* and *since* **P** *has, have, for, since* **V** *work* + preposition **S** listening for inference

LISTENING

A Work in groups. Complete the tips for job interviews with *do* or *don't*.

1 __________ eat smelly food or smoke before the interview.

2 __________ arrive ten minutes before your appointment.

3 __________ listen carefully to introductions and try to remember names.

4 __________ answer your phone or check messages during the interview.

5 __________ be negative about yourself or your last job.

6 __________ ask one or two questions at the end.

5.6 **B LISTEN FOR GIST** Barry has a job interview with Gemma. Listen and choose the summary (1–3) that best describes the interview.

1 The interview goes well. Gemma and Barry have a good conversation. Barry will probably get the job.

2 The interview goes fairly well. Barry has a lot of experience working on a team. Barry might get the job.

3 The interview does not go well. Barry lies. Gemma is annoyed. Barry will definitely not get the job.

Glossary

call center (n) a place where a large number of people are employed to deal with customers by telephone, either in order to sell something or to answer questions

résumé (n) a document giving details of your certifications and the jobs you have had in the past that you send to someone when you are applying for a job

teamwork (n) work that you do together with other people

telemarketing (n) the activity or job of using the telephone to sell goods or services

5.6 **C** Test your memory! Check (✓) the things Barry has done and put an ✗ on the things he has not. Listen and check.

1 worked in a call center ☐

2 worked on a team ☐

3 worked for a telemarketing company ☐

4 been skydiving ☐

5 read French poetry ☐

5.7 **D** Listen to three extracts from the interview. Then answer the questions about each extract. Use the information in the box to help you.

Listening for inference

When you listen to a foreign language, use vocabulary and context clues and your wider knowledge to figure out the meaning of what you hear.

Think about the speaker's tone and attitude, as well as what they don't say.

Extract one

1 Does Barry check whether he needs to tell the truth? *yes / no*

2 Does he give a real example? *yes / no*

3 Do you think he has ever worked as part of a team? *yes / no*

Extract two

4 Is Barry interested in skydiving? *yes / no*

5 Does he think it's exciting? *yes / no*

6 Do you think he has ever actually done it? *yes / no*

Extract three

7 Does Barry remember what he wrote on his résumé? *yes / no*

8 Does he tell the truth about what he wrote on his résumé? *yes / no*

9 Do you think he enjoys French poetry? *yes / no*

E SPEAK Work in groups. Have you ever had an interview for a job, course or scholarship? Tell your group about it.

GRAMMAR

Present perfect with *for* and *since*

A WORK IT OUT Look at the sentences from Barry's interview and answer the questions.

I left my old job in June.

1 Does Barry still do his old job?
2 Is the action *leave* finished or unfinished?
3 What tense is the verb *leave* in?

I've worked at the call center for six weeks.

4 Does Barry still work at the call center?
5 Is the action *work* finished or unfinished?
6 What tense is the verb *work* in?

B Choose the correct words to complete the rules.

Present perfect and simple past

1 We use the ***present perfect / simple past*** to talk about actions or situations that started and finished in the past.
2 We use the ***present perfect / simple past*** to talk about actions or situations that started in the past, but are unfinished and so continue until the present.

C Look at the words in **bold** in the sentences from Barry's interview. Complete the rules with *how long*, *for* or *since*.

How long *have you worked there?*

Actually, I've been here ***since*** *9 am.*

You've been here ***for*** *three hours?*

Present perfect with *how long*, *for* and *since*

1 We use __________ + present perfect to ask about the duration of an action.
2 We use __________ to talk about the point in time when something started, e.g. *yesterday, I was young.*
3 We use __________ + present perfect to talk about a length of time until the present time, e.g. *three hours, two weeks.*

D Look at the sentence from Barry's interview and choose the correct words to complete the rule.

I've liked skydiving since I was a teenager.

since

After *since* we usually use a verb in ***present perfect / simple past***.

E Go to the **Grammar Hub** on **page XIV**.

PRONUNCIATION

has, have, for, since

5.8 Listen and repeat.

1 How long has he lived there?
2 How long have you worked there?
3 He's lived there for three years.
4 I've worked there since last summer.

VOCABULARY

work + preposition

A Go to the **Vocabulary Hub** on **page XXI**.

B SPEAK Work as a class. Talk to as many different people as possible in five minutes about their job or the job of someone they know. Write notes for each person you talk to.

Cassie: She works in IT for a software company. She's a computer programmer. She works in their office in the center of the city.

C SPEAK Work in pairs. Compare your notes. Which jobs were the most unusual or interesting?

SPEAKING HUB

A You are going to talk about a topic in which you are an expert. Consider the following areas:

- your profession and/or studies
- a skill you've learned, e.g. cooking, skiing, car mechanics, piano

B PLAN Think of some questions you could ask your classmates about their topics.

How long ...?
What can/can't you do?

C DISCUSS Work in a group. Interview each student in your group about their expertise. What were the most interesting things you learned about your classmates?

Answer questions on topics in which you are an expert

5.4 The cat

F– give information about your work experience in a job interview
P– singular and plural forms

COMPREHENSION

A SPEAK Work in pairs. Look at the pictures above from Neena's job interview. What do you think goes wrong in the interview? Watch the video and check.

B 03:09–05:00 Watch the last part of the interview again. Answer the questions.

1 Whose cat was it?
2 What was the cat's name?
3 What is Neena doing on Monday?

C 00:27–03:06 Complete the job interview form for Neena. Then watch part of the video again and check your answers.

JOBS, JOBS, JOBS AND JOBS

Job interview

Name: *Neena Patel*
Current job: Working for a [1]__________ firm.
Responsible for international [2]__________.
Time in current job: [3]__________ years.
Reasons for changing job: Is looking for a [4]__________ challenge.
Strengths: Is good at working [5]__________ pressure. Can [6]__________ her time.
Is very organized. Is good at [7]__________ management. Works well on a [8]__________.
Weaknesses: Is a perfectionist – enjoys getting everything [9]__________.
A good candidate for the job: [10] Yes / No

MILLY

SAM

NEENA

ZAC

GABY

FUNCTIONAL LANGUAGE

Give information about your work experience in a job interview

A Cross out the word that is NOT possible to complete the sentences.

1 Currently, I'm working for *a law firm* / *Citibank* / ~~*architect*~~.

2 I have to manage *a team* / *five sales representatives* / *a company car*.

3 I've worked there for *last year* / *a long time* / *four years*.

4 People say I'm good at *working under pressure* / *manage my time* / *my job*.

5 I've learned how to *manage my time* / *working on a team* / *deal with clients*.

6 I work well *on a team* / *under pressure* / *my job*.

B Look at Exercise A. Think of another word for each sentence to replace the one you crossed out.

USEFUL PHRASES

A Complete the conversations with the useful phrases in the box. Then watch the video again and check your answers.

Go on. How did it go? It was going so well … Just go! Let me think. Please take a seat. Tell me about yourself. That's a good question.

Gaby:	1 ________
Neena:	Oh, Gaby, it was awful.
Gaby:	What happened?
Neena:	2 ________
Interviewer:	Good afternoon, Neena. 3 ________
	So Neena, 4 ________
	What have you learned from your current job?
Neena:	5 ________
Interviewer:	And any weak points?
Neena:	6 ________
	Well, I have one question.
Interviewer:	7 ________
Neena:	So, will you call me?
Interviewer:	8 ________

B How do you say these useful phrases in your language?

PRONUNCIATION

Singular and plural forms

5.9 **A** Listen and repeat the singular and plural forms of the nouns in the box. Which noun has an extra syllable in the plural form?

account(s) challenge(s) job(s) perfectionist(s) pressure(s) project(s) question(s) strength(s)

B **SPEAK** Work in pairs. Practice saying the words in Exercise A. Listen and check your partner's pronunciation.

SPEAKING

A Think about the things you are good at. Write down three strengths and one weakness. Then work in pairs and compare your ideas.

B Work in pairs. Write down three important skills for each of the jobs in the box.

accountant soccer team manager teacher website manager

C Role-play a job interview. Use the job interview form in Comprehension Exercise C to help you. Include at least two useful phrases. Take turns.

Student A: Choose a job from Exercise B and interview Student B for the job.

Student B: Answer Student A's questions.

Student A: Decide if Student B is suitable for the job.

Give information about your work experience in a job interview

➤ Turn to **page XXVIII** to learn how to write a cover email.

Unit 5 Review

VOCABULARY

A Match beginnings of the sentences (1–5) with the ends of the sentences (a–e).

1 What advantages are there to a job where you work
2 How important do you think it is to earn
3 What are the disadvantages of being
4 When did you last take
5 Do you think people should get

a a day off from work or school and what did you do?
b shifts, so sometimes you start at night or early in the morning?
c a pay raise every year or only when they have done well at work?
d your own boss?
e a high salary in your job?

B Write the missing words to complete the sentences.

1 My brother is very **c**___ ___ ___; he always looks good.
2 She's not allowed to wear **c**___ ___ ___ ___ ___ clothes to work.
3 I love those high-heeled shoes – they have a very **s**___ ___ ___ ___ ___ ___ design.
4 I don't like that T-shirt. I don't think those colors look **a**___ ___ ___ ___ ___ ___ ___ ___ ___ ___ .
5 In our country, you must wear **d**___ ___ ___ ___ clothes to a wedding.

C Choose the correct prepositions. In three examples, both are possible.

1 They work *at* / *for* the IT department.
2 He works *in* / *at* marketing.
3 She works *at* / *for* Bluemoon Software Services.
4 She works *at* / *for* an advertising firm.
5 I work *at* / *in* a library.
6 We work *in* / *for* a telemarketing company.

GRAMMAR

A Choose the best words to complete the sentences.

1 When I was young, I *can* / *could* stay up late, but these days I get tired early.
2 I really enjoy *being able to* / *can* work for myself.
3 Johann *able to* / *can* speak four languages.
4 I *was able to* / *could* speak to my boss last Friday about getting a pay raise.
5 I'd like *can* / *to be able to* speak perfect English one day.

B Match the rules (1–8) with the meanings (a–d).

Memo: Information for palace staff

1 ___ You can park your car in the staff parking lot.
2 ___ You must not bring your own cell phone inside the palace.
3 ___ You can't take any pictures while at work.
4 ___ You have to be nicely dressed at all times.*
5 ___ You must call the Queen 'Your Majesty'.
6 ___ You must not mention anything you see or hear at work to anyone.
7 ___ You can smoke in the staff smoking area.
8 ___ *If the Royal family are away, you don't have to wear the full uniform.

a This is necessary or is a rule.
b This is not necessary but allowed.
c This is allowed but not necessary.
d This is not allowed.

C Complete the conversations with the simple past or present perfect form of the verbs in parentheses.

Erin: How long [1] ________________ (*you / work*) here?
Paulie: Oh, not long. [2] ________________ (*I / start*) work last December. But, you see that lady there? Well, [3] ________________ (*she / be*) here for 20 years. [4] ________________ (*she / become*) a cook when she was only 17.

Karl: I thought you worked for a newspaper? When [5] ________________ (*you / change*) jobs?
Crystal: Years ago! [6] ________________ (*I / not work*) in journalism since about 2004.

Pippa: [7] ________________ (*I / want*) to be a doctor when I was a child, but now I'm a vet.
Gianni: A vet? That's so cool. [8] ________________ (*I / love*) animals since I was little.

FUNCTIONAL LANGUAGE

A Complete the phrases to use in job interviews with the words in the box.

enjoy	learned	problem	question	responsible	team

1 I've ________________ how to motivate other people.
2 Well, I have one ________________ I'd like to ask.
3 I'm ________________ for customer service.
4 I ________________ working in a busy office.
5 I work well on a ________________.
6 Well, I have a ________________ with the weekend hours.

6 HEALTH

> Health is not valued until sickness comes.
>
> Thomas Fuller

Yoga enthusiasts take part in the annual Times Square event celebrating the Summer Solstice, the longest day of the year, New York.

OBJECTIVES

- give a presentation on health dos and don'ts
- plan an exercise event for your local community
- encourage people to make a lifestyle change
- talk about your symptoms at a pharmacy
- write a product review

Work with a partner. Discuss the questions.

1 What do you do to stay healthy?
2 Read the quote. Do you agree with it?
3 Would you like to take part in an event like the one in the picture? Why/Why not?

6.1 Health myths

Give a presentation on health dos and don'ts

G quantifiers *too* and *enough* V minor illnesses P /ʌ/, /ɔː/, /uː/, /eɪ/ and /ɜː/

LISTENING

A Match the definitions (1–7) with the words in the box.

a balanced diet antibiotics confused expert liquid myth reality

1 something that people wrongly believe to be true
2 someone who has a particular skill or who knows a lot about a particular subject
3 a fact, event or situation as it really exists
4 a range of food that a person eats to provide all the good things their body needs
5 drugs that cure illnesses and infections caused by bacteria
6 unable to understand something or think clearly about it
7 a substance (such as water) that can flow, has no fixed shape and is not a solid or a gas

B SPEAK Work in pairs. Check (✓) the sentences about health you have heard before. Which ones do you think are true and which ones are myths? Give reasons.

1 Everyone should drink eight glasses of water per day. ☐
2 Eating fatty food makes you fat. ☐
3 Eggs are bad for your heart. ☐
4 Cold weather causes colds. ☐
5 Take antibiotics when you have a cold. ☐

6.1 **C LISTEN FOR GIST** Look at the glossary. Then listen to the introduction of *Live with Pippa* and answer the questions.

Glossary

calorie (n) unit for measuring how much energy you get from food
carbohydrate (n) a substance found in foods such as sugar, bread and potatoes. Carbohydrates supply your body with heat and energy.
fatty (adj) containing a lot of fat
virus (n) a thing that can enter your body and make you sick

1 How many experts does Pippa speak to?
2 Choose the best summary of Pippa's message in the introduction to the show.
   a It is better to ask a medical professional than look online for information about health.
   b It is difficult to know which online information about health is true.
   c Bad online advice about health is making healthy people sick.

6.1 **D LISTEN FOR DETAIL** Listen again and choose a, b or c.

1 Doctor Singh says that …
   a most headaches are due to a lack of water.
   b we get some of the water we need from our food.
   c more than eight glasses of water per day is dangerous.
2 Michael says that …
   a everyone needs some fat in their diets.
   b most people get fat because they eat too much sugar.
   c we shouldn't eat fatty food.
3 Dr. Tremblay says you are more likely to catch a cold or flu …
   a if you spend time outside in cold weather.
   b if you don't get enough vitamins in your diet.
   c if you spend time indoors with a lot of people.
4 Lia says that …
   a advice on eating eggs changes regularly.
   b advice on eating eggs is not the same as it was in the past.
   c advice on eating eggs is the same as it has always been.

GRAMMAR

Quantifiers *too* and *enough*

A WORK IT OUT Complete the sentences from the radio show (1–5) using the audio script on page XXXIV. Then match the sentences with the rules (a–c).

1 You drink too ____________ coffee. rule ___
2 You don't sleep ____________. rule ___
3 It's because you go to bed ____________ early. rule ___
4 Make sure you are getting ____________ vitamins. rule ___
5 Too ____________ eggs are bad for your heart. rule ___

Quantifiers *too* and *enough*

a We use *too* + adjective or adverb, *too much* and *too many* to mean more than the right amount.
b We use *enough* to mean the right amount.
c We use *not enough* to mean less than the right amount.

B Look at the sentences from the radio show in Exercise A and complete the rules.

too much* and *too many

1 We use *too much* / *too many* with countable nouns.
2 We use *too much* / *too many* with uncountable nouns.

C Go to the **Grammar Hub** on **page XVI**.

D **PRACTICE** Complete the sentences so they are true for you.

1 I spend too much time ______________ and not enough time ______________.
2 I eat too much/many ______________ and not enough ______________.
3 I don't ______________ enough and I ______________ too much/often.
4 I find ______________ too difficult.
5 I have enough ______________, but not enough ______________.

E **SPEAK** Work in pairs. Discuss your answers to Exercise D.

VOCABULARY
Minor illnesses

A Read Dr. Tremblay's audio script on **page XXXIV** and underline six health problems he talks about.

B Label the pictures (1–10) with the health problems in the box.

a broken bone ~~a cold~~ a cough
a headache a temperature a sore throat
flu stomachache sunburn toothache

PRONUNCIATION
/ʌ/, /ɔː/, /uː/, /eɪ/ and /ɜː/

6.2 **A** Listen and repeat.

1 /ʌ/ but
2 /ɔː/ caught
3 /uː/ do
4 /eɪ/ pay
5 /ɜː/ fur

6.3 **B** Each word contains one of the sounds in Exercise A. Listen and match the words with the sounds. Then underline the letter(s) that make the sounds.

1 burn
2 ache
3 stomach
4 flu
5 sore

a /ʌ/
b /ɔː/
c /uː/
d /eɪ/
e /ɜː/

C **SPEAK** Work in pairs. What do people usually do for each of the problems in Vocabulary Exercise B? Use ideas below to help you and your own ideas.

- go to bed
- take medicine
- go to the doctor
- take painkillers
- put on lotion
- stay home from work

SPEAKING

A Work in pairs. Plan and give a short presentation called *The dos and don'ts of staying active and healthy.*

B Write a list of dos and don'ts for each of the topics:

- food and drink
- sleep
- exercise
- stress
- avoiding and recovering from illness

C Present your advice to the class. Ask them to guess which piece of advice is a myth or bad advice.

1

a cold

2

____

3

____

4

____

5

____

6

____

7
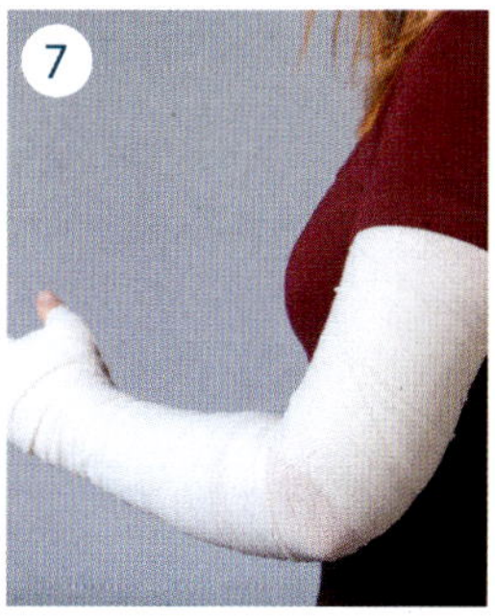
____

8

____

9

____

10
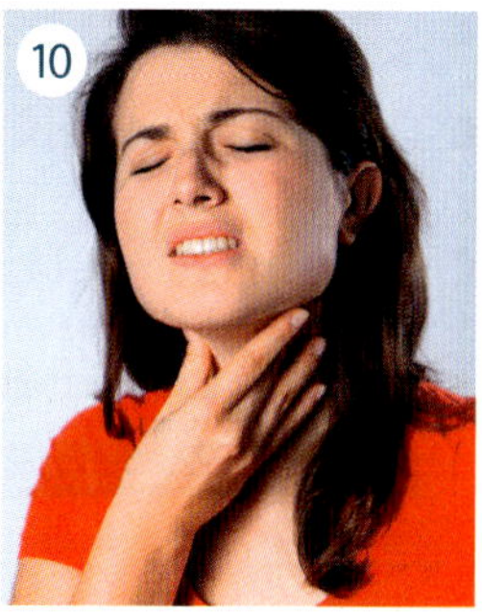
____

Give a presentation on health dos and don'ts

6.2 Keep fit

Plan an exercise event for your local community

V exercise   P /ŋ/, /n/ and /m/   G *-ing* forms

VOCABULARY

Exercise

A Work in pairs. Make a list of different ways of exercising. You have one minute.

Walking, swimming …

B Go to the **Vocabulary Hub** on **page XXI**.

C **SPEAK** Look at the **Vocabulary Hub** Exercise B on **page XXI**. Go around the class and ask the questions. If someone answers *yes*, write their name and ask a follow-up question.

A: Do you hate working out at the gym?
B: Yes, I do.
A: Why?
B: I like to exercise outdoors and I don't like to exercise with so many other people watching me. I find most gyms too busy.

PRONUNCIATION

/ŋ/, /n/ and /m/

6.4 **A** Listen to these sounds. Do they sound the same or different?

1 /ŋ/ biking   2 /n/ run   3 /m/ team

6.4 **B** Listen again and repeat the sounds.

6.5 **C** Listen and complete the table with the words you hear. Do the words have an /ŋ/, /n/ or /m/ sound? Some words have more than one of the sounds.

/ŋ/	/n/	/m/

READING

A Check (✓) the sentences you agree with. Then work in pairs and explain your choices.

- Running is great exercise and great fun. ☐
- I'd like to run a marathon one day. ☐
- I prefer team sports, like racquetball or field hockey. ☐
- Jogging is exercise, not fun. ☐
- Running is boring. ☐
- The only time I run is to catch the bus. ☐

B **SCAN** Read texts 1–3. What is the purpose of each?

Text ___: to inform   Text ___: to persuade

Text ___: to entertain

1

Funny fitness

Did you know that laughing for 15 minutes can burn up to 40 calories? We hope these jokes and quotes will keep you smiling as you walk to the store, jog around the park or run your next marathon.

Q What is a runner's favorite school subject?
A Jog-raphy

'If you are in a bad mood, go for a walk. If you are still in a bad mood, go for another walk.'
Hippocrates

Patient: Doctor, can you give me something to stop sleepwalking?
Doctor: I'm afraid I can't, sir. You need the exercise!

2

Parkrun

Are you looking for an easy way to stay in shape and lose weight? Would you like to run 5 km in a family-friendly atmosphere? Would you like to compare your results with other runners from all over the world? If so, then check out *Parkrun*.

Parkrun organizes free weekly timed runs in parks all over the world. The 5 km runs take place on weekend mornings and are open to everyone. After each race, runners receive detailed results via email.

Parkrun is an international community of over one million runners in 17 countries and there is always space for more! So come and join the *Parkrun* family and get fit for free!

Glossary

atmosphere (n) the mood or feeling in a place

3

MARATHON MAN

What do you think it takes to become a running master? Fauja Singh, from east London, finished a 10 km race in Hong Kong in one hour and 32 minutes – and he did it at the age of 101.

In 2011, Singh became the oldest person to run a marathon. At 100 years of age, he completed the Toronto Marathon in just over eight hours.

As a young man, Mr. Singh was a farmer in Punjab, India. Then in the 1960s, he went to live in Britain and only began running when he was 89 years old.

Mr. Singh plans to run again for charity, but the Hong Kong 10 km was his final competitive race. 'I will remember this day. I will miss it,' Mr. Singh said after the event.

C READ FOR DETAIL Read again and answer the questions. Write *Funny fitness* (FF), *Parkrun* (PR), *Marathon man* (MM) or none of the texts (N).

Which text …

1 tells the story of an individual? ____
2 offers readers the chance to read more online? ____
3 tries to sell readers something? ____
4 reports the results of a research project? ____
5 tries to make readers laugh? ____
6 describes the purpose of a particular organization? ____

D SPEAK Work in pairs. Discuss the questions.

1 Why is running such a popular form of exercise?
2 Would you like to do a parkrun? Why/Why not?

GRAMMAR

-ing forms

A Look at the examples of different *-ing* forms used in the texts. Then complete the rules with the words in the box.

1 Did you know that **laughing** for 15 minutes can burn up to 40 calories? (gerund)
2 Are you **looking** for an easy way to stay in shape and lose weight? (present participle)
3 What do you think it takes to become a **running** master? (adjective)

adjectives | gerunds | present participle

***-ing* forms**

1 We use the ______________ *-ing* form with the verb *to be* to talk about things that are happening now or around now, and are not finished.
2 We use *-ing* form as ______________ to describe nouns.
3 We use *-ing* form as ______________ to make nouns.

B Go to the **Grammar Hub** on **page XVI**.

C SPEAK Work in pairs. Discuss the questions.

1 What is your favorite form of exercise?
2 Do you like working out? Why/Why not?

SPEAKING

A Work in groups. Plan an event to encourage local people to start doing more exercise. Think about:

- who your event is for
- how it will help people get in shape or start exercising
- what people need to bring to the event
- how you will promote the event

B Describe your event to the rest of the class. Which event is the most popular. Why?

Plan an exercise event for your local community

6.3 We may never 'meat' again

Encourage people to make a lifestyle change

G present perfect with *just, already* and *yet* **V** food groups **P** /s/ and /ʃ/ **S** scanning for key words

READING

A Match the words in the box to pictures (1–6).

avocado broccoli fur grain kale wheat

B **READ FOR GIST** Read *A fresh start*. Which three reasons for going vegetarian or vegan are given in the article?

1 

2 

3 

4 

5 

6 

A fresh start

Large numbers of people are saying 'never again!' to meat and becoming vegetarian or vegan. For some it's about health, for others it's about concern for the environment. Whatever the reason, many people are changing the way they eat forever.

Research by the Vegan Society states that in 2016 there were around 542,000 vegans in the UK alone. Veganism is also on the rise thanks to celebrity supporters including Ellie Goulding, Liam Hemsworth and Venus and Serena Williams.

There are various reasons why people decide to go vegetarian or vegan. Some do it for their health. Vegans get all the vitamins, minerals and other things they need for a balanced diet from grains, fruits, seeds, nuts and vegetables such as kale, broccoli, beans and avocados. A vegetarian diet can help people lose weight because it is low in fat. High-fat diets are linked to serious health problems including diabetes, heart disease and cancer.

Some people give up meat because they are worried about the environment. A 2006 FAO (The Food and Agriculture Organization of the United Nations) study reported that 18 percent of greenhouse gases come from farm animals such as cows, sheep and chickens. That's more than all of the world's cars, trains and planes put together. We use over 36 percent of the world's grain to feed farm animals, yet a quarter of the people in the world do not have enough food. If we made food for people from the grain instead, there would be enough for everyone.

Other people go meat-free because they feel it is wrong to kill animals. Animals feel pain and fear. Many farmed animals are kept in poor conditions with little space and no time outdoors. In the UK, around 990 million farmed animals are killed for food each year.

With so many grocery stores and restaurants now offering vegetarian and vegan goods, it's easier than ever to give up or reduce the amount of meat we eat. Why not try a few meat-free days a week – you could help reduce world hunger and even help with climate change!

Are you vegan or vegetarian?

We want your comments!

Nora_27: **I've just changed to a vegetarian diet after years of eating meat.** It's only been a week, but I feel much healthier and I highly recommend it!

M-M-Maxine: I feel bad about killing animals, but I really enjoy meat. **I've already eaten two sausages and a chicken sandwich today, and it's only lunchtime!** I don't think I'd last very long without meat.

Cool_keith2: **I've been vegetarian for a while, but I haven't managed to go vegan yet.** It seems like a lot of work to plan and prepare the food. Any advice?

Kellykale: Great article. Vegan food is great! **Have you tried kale chips yet?** They are really tasty and great as a healthy snack.

Glossary

billion (number) the number 1,000,000,000

greenhouse gas (n) a gas that stops heat from escaping the atmosphere and causes the greenhouse effect, the gas that makes global warming worse

mineral (n) a natural substance in some foods that you need for good health, for example, iron and calcium

vitamin (n) natural substances found in food that are necessary to keep your body healthy

C SCAN Read again. Are the sentences true (T) or false (F)? Use the information in the box to help you.

Scanning for key words

When you are reading to find specific information, such as names, dates and statistics, move your eyes quickly over the text and look for titles, numbers, symbols and names. Read around these items to find the information you are looking for. This is called scanning.

Scanning helps save time in exams and is useful for previewing texts to decide whether to read them in more detail.

1 There are about half a million vegetarians in the UK. *T / F*
2 A fair number of famous people are vegans. *T / F*
3 Vegans need to take extra vitamins to stay healthy. *T / F*
4 Vehicles produce less air pollution than farming animals for meat. *T / F*
5 If we produced less meat, there would be more food for those people who do not have enough. *T / F*
6 It is difficult to buy vegan products. *T / F*

D SPEAK Work in pairs. What are the arguments for and against farming and killing animals for food?

GRAMMAR

Present perfect with *just*, *already* and *yet*

A WORK IT OUT Look at the sentences in **bold** in the comments section of *A fresh start*. Then complete the rules with *just*, *already* or *yet*.

Present perfect with *just*, *already* and *yet*

1 We use the present perfect with ______________ in positive statements to say something happened very recently.
2 We use the present perfect with ______________ in positive statements to say that something happened before now or earlier than expected.
3 We use the present perfect with ______________:
- in negative statements to say that something hasn't happened, but it still might.
- in questions to ask if something has happened.

B Look again and choose the correct words to complete the rules.

1 *Just* comes ***before / after*** the past participle in a sentence.
2 *Already* usually comes ***before / after*** the past participle in a sentence.
3 *Yet* comes at the ***beginning / end*** of a sentence or question.

C Go to the **Grammar Hub** on **page XVI**.

D SPEAK. Work in pairs. Have you done any exercise today? Make true sentences with present perfect and *just*, *already* or *yet*.

VOCABULARY

Food groups

A Work in pairs. Make a list of different food items. You have one minute.

B Go to the **Vocabulary Hub** on **page XXI**.

C SPEAK Work in pairs. Have you eaten any healthy food today? Who has been kinder to their body?

I had two oranges with my breakfast, and I've just eaten an apple and two kiwis, so I've had five pieces of fruit today already.

PRONUNCIATION

/s/ and /ʃ/

A SPEAK Work in pairs. Write the words in the box in the correct place. Use the examples to help you.

chefs fish fresh lettuce ~~lobster~~ rice sandwich sauce spinach sushi ~~sugar~~

/s/	/ʃ/	/s/ and /ʃ/
lobster	*sugar*	

6.6 **B** Listen and check. Then listen again and repeat the words.

C SPEAK Work in pairs. Student A – point to a word in Exercise B. Student B – say the word. Take turns.

SPEAKING HUB

A Work in groups. You are going to design a leaflet to help other students make a lifestyle change. Choose one of the following:

- eat less meat
- stop drinking bottled water
- use more fresh ingredients when cooking
- eat less sugar

B PLAN What information will you include on the leaflet? Think about the areas below and then design your leaflet.

- health benefits
- environmental benefits
- how your school or college will help
- how you or someone you know changed their lifestyle in this way and how they benefited

C REFLECT Read the other groups' leaflets. Which do you think would be most successful and why?

Encourage people to make a lifestyle change

6.4 Painful experience

F – talk about your symptoms at a pharmacy
P – vowel sounds

COMPREHENSION

A ▶ 00:00–02:13 Watch the first part of the video without sound and answer the questions.

1 How does the pharmacist feel?

2 How does Gaby feel?

3 Check (✓) the parts of their bodies that hurt.

arm	☐	back	☐	ears	☐	eyes	☐	foot	☐
hand	☐	head	☐	leg	☐	nose	☐	throat	☐

B ▶ 00:00–02:13 Watch the first part of the video again with sound and check your answers to Exercise A.

C **SPEAK** Work in pairs. What advice would you give Gaby? What advice would you give the pharmacist?

D ▶ 02:26–04:54 Watch the second part of the video and check your answers to Exercise C.

FUNCTIONAL LANGUAGE

Talk about your symptoms at a pharmacy

A Write the headings in the box in the correct place (a–c).

Explain symptoms | Ask about health | Give advice

Useful language

a ____________

Are you OK?
Are you [1] ____________?
What's painful?
What are your symptoms?
Do you have anything for a sore throat / a [2] ____________?
Do you have sore eyes / [3] ____________?
Are you allergic to anything?

b ____________

It's very painful.
My nose / [4] ____________ hurts.
I'm not feeling very well.
I have a terrible cold.
You don't have a cold, you have hay fever / [5] ____________.

c ____________

I suggest these tablets / [6] ____________.
Take one every eight hours.
You could try drinking a hot lemon and honey.
I think you should rest / [7] ____________.

MILLY

SAM

NEENA

ZAC

GABY

B Write the words and phrases in the box in the correct place in Exercise A.

back flu a temperature headache relax sure you're OK this medicine

USEFUL PHRASES

A Match the useful phrases (1–6) with similar phrases which show the meaning (a–f).

1	I know how you feel.	**a**	A lot of people get this in the summer.
2	We are both not very well today.	**b**	Don't I need more?
3	It's common at this time of year.	**c**	I have the same symptoms as you.
4	I'll be fine.	**d**	It's my favorite cure.
5	Is one enough?	**e**	You and I are sick today.
6	That usually makes me feel better.	**f**	Don't worry about me.

B How do you say these useful phrases in your language?

PRONUNCIATION

Vowel sounds

A Match the words which have the same vowel sound.

1	cough	**a**	allergic
2	hurt	**b**	door
3	pain	**c**	nose
4	sore	**d**	same
5	throat	**e**	wrong

6.7 **B** Listen and check. Then listen again and repeat the words.

C **SPEAK** Work in pairs. Practice saying the words. Listen and check your partner's pronunciation.

SPEAKING

Work in pairs. Role-play a conversation about health. Take turns being Student A and Student B.

Student A: Choose an ailment from the pictures and explain the symptoms.

You must use the following words: *feeling*, *have*, *hurt*(*s*), *painful*.

Student B: Ask questions and give advice.

You must use the following words: *allergic*, *take*, *temperature*, *try*.

Talk about your symptoms at a pharmacy

➤ Turn to **page XXIX** to learn how to write a product review.

Unit 6 Review

VOCABULARY

A Complete the crossword.

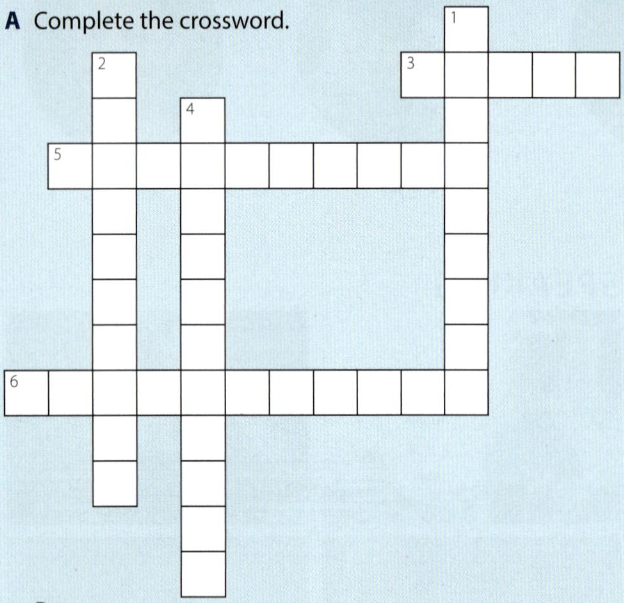

Down

1 See the dentist with this problem.

2 Leg, arm, finger? Go to the hospital. (two words)

4 You are warmer than you should be.

Across

3 Cover your mouth with your hand when you do this.

5 Try not to talk. Drink hot drinks. Suck a candy. (two words)

6 Did you eat too much?

B What are the missing words? Choose a, b or c to complete the survey.

WELCOME TO *SUNNY'S GYM*

Check (✓) your fitness goals.

1 ___ weight ☐

2 get or ___ in shape ☐

Do you …

3 ___ at a gym? ☐

4 ___ jogging? ☐

5 ___ a team sport? ☐

6 ___ yoga? ☐

	a	b	c
1	get	put	lose
2	stay	work	go
3	work it	work out	work on
4	run	do	go
5	go	play	join
6	play	go	do

C Choose the correct words to complete the sentences.

1 Pasta is made from *nuts* / *wheat*.

2 You can eat the shell of *shrimp* / *lobster*, but a lot of people choose not to.

3 Pizza is made with bread, cheese and *avocado* / *tomato* sauce.

4 British-style fish and chips usually includes *tuna* / *cod*.

5 One of the main salad ingredients is *rice* / *lettuce*.

GRAMMAR

A Complete the sentences with *too many*, *too much* and *not enough*.

1 We can't make a cake today. There are ________ eggs in the fridge.

2 There are ________ flavors of ice cream – I can't decide!

3 There are ________ chairs here. I'll get two more from the kitchen.

4 We shouldn't eat ________ sugar in our diets. It's unhealthy.

5 I've eaten ________ pie. I don't feel well.

B Write the word in parentheses in the correct place. Then circle the correct *-ing* form. Choose gerund (G), adjective (A) or present participle (PP).

1 She left the gym because of the prices. (*rising*) *G / A / PP*

2 Lucien is very fit these days. (*becoming*) *G / A / PP*

3 He isn't any exercise right now. (*doing*) *G / A / PP*

4 My brother loves marathons. (*running*) *G / A / PP*

5 I want to try yoga by myself. (*practicing*) *G / A / PP*

C Complete the comments from a health website with *just*, *already* or *yet*.

HART_27: I became vegetarian about two weeks ago. I feel lighter and I have clearer skin [1]________. I've [2]________ weighed myself but I haven't lost any weight [3]________.

KENNYKEN: This morning, I finally decided to go vegan. I've [4]________ come back from the store with vegan ingredients and a cookbook. Actually, I have one vegan cookbook [5]________, but I haven't made anything from it [6]________.

FUNCTIONAL LANGUAGE

A Complete the words in the conversation at a pharmacy.

Pharmacist: Good morning. [1]H___ ___ can I h___ ___ ___ ?

Customer: Oh, good morning. [2]I f___ ___ ___ terr___ ___ ___ ___ ___ .

Pharmacist: [3]Wh___ ___ are your sym___ ___ ___ ___ ___ ?

Customer: [4]I ha___ ___ a s___ ___ ___ thr___ ___ ___ and a cou___ ___ . [5]It really hu___ ___ ___ .

Pharmacist: Oh, dear. Anything else?

Customer: Well, I think [6]I ha___ ___ a tem___ ___ ___ ___ ___ ___ ___ ___ ___, too, because I feel hot all the time.

Endmatter Contents

Grammar Hub

1.1 Question forms

Questions with *do* / *does* / *did*

Do/Does/Did + subject + infinitive
Do you have children?
Does he go to English classes?
Did she write a blog post?
Did they do their homework?

- We use the auxiliary verb (*do, does, did*), without a question word, to ask yes/no questions.

Question words

Question word + *do/does/did* + subject + infinitive
What do you say to a stranger?
Where does he come from?
What did you say to your colleague?
Where did she study psychology?

- We use *What* to ask about things and *Where* to ask about places.

Questions with *be*

Am/Is/Are + subject
Am I in this class?
Are they strangers?

Am/Is/Are + subject + *-ing*
Is she doing her homework now?
Are you having fun?

Was/Were + subject
Was he a sensible person?
Were they good at English?

- We use questions with *be*, without a question word, to ask yes/no questions.
- We can also ask questions with *What*, *Where*, *When*, *Why* and *Who* before the verb *be*.

Questions with the present perfect

Have/Has + subject + past participle
Have you visited that website?
Has he written a bucket list?

- We use present perfect questions, without a question word, to ask yes/no questions.
- We use *ever* to ask about life experiences.

  *Have you **ever** met a famous person?*
- We can also ask question with *What*, *Where*, *When*, *Why* and *Who* before the verb *have*.

1.2 Frequency words and phrases

0% ⟵⟶ 100%

never rarely occasionally sometimes often normally always

- We use frequency words after *be* and *can*.

  *He is **normally** very sensible.*

  *I can **never** read your handwriting!*
- We use frequency words before other verbs.

  *I **sometimes** watch vlogs online.*

once twice three times	a	day week month year
every so often	now and then	most of the time

- We usually use frequency phrases at the beginning or end of the sentence.

  *I take my dog for a walk **twice a day**.*

  ***Every so often**, I travel to another country.*

1.3 Indefinite pronouns

	-one	*-body*	*-thing*	*-where*
every-	everyone	everybody	everything	everywhere
any-	anyone	anybody	anything	anywhere
some-	someone	somebody	something	somewhere
no-	no one	nobody	nothing	nowhere

- We use the ending *-body* or *-one* with people. They have the same meaning.

  *Every**body** loved the party. OR Every**one** loved the party.*
- We use the ending *-thing* with objects.

  *I always take some**thing** to read on the train.*
- We use the ending *-where* with places.

  *They live some**where** in Italy.*
- We use *any-* in negative sentences.

  *I don't know **any**thing.*
- We also use *any-* in questions.

  *Is there **any**thing unusual about her handwriting?*

Be careful!

- With offers, we can also use *some-* in questions.

  *Do you want **some**thing to eat?*
- We use indefinite pronouns with singular verbs.

  *Everyone **is** interested. NOT ~~Everyone are interested.~~*
- We use *'s* with indefinite pronouns for possessives.

  Is this anybody's cell phone?

1.1 Question forms

A Put the words in order to make questions.

1 you / do / go / skiing / want / to

Do you want to go skiing?

2 does / what / do / he / weekends / on

______

3 did / you / meet / where / for coffee

______

4 you / tea / are / coffee / or / drinking

______

5 your / new colleagues / were / at the office

______

6 you / been / have / ever / Mexico / to

______

7 tried / that / she / has / new restaurant

______

B Correct the mistakes in each sentence.

1 Why ~~you~~ did you did choose that topic?
2 Have you ever meet a graphologist?
3 What you are talking about?
4 Did they went to the movie theater last night?
5 Where you did put the new keyboard?
6 What your best friend's name is?
7 Did you anything nice last weekend?

➤ Go back to page 3.

1.2 Frequency words and phrases

A Write the missing letters.

1 I n_e_ _v_ _e_r get bored writing my blog.
2 She's s_ _ _ _ _ _ _ _s late for work.
3 They a_ _ _ _ _ _ watch vlogs in their free time.
4 We're n_ _ _ _ _ _ _y home before 11.
5 He o_ _ _ _ _ _ _ _ _ _ _y checks his social media accounts at work.
6 I r_ _ _ _ _ _ go online before starting work.
7 He r_ _ _ _ _ _ _ _ visits his relatives in Italy.

B Put the words and phrases of frequency in the correct place in each sentence. Sometimes more than one answer is possible.

1 We go on vacation. (*once a year*)

We go on vacation once a year.

2 They comment on online articles. (*now and then*)

______

3 I read online tips. (*every so often*)

______

4 She writes for popular magazines. (*most of the time*)

______

5 He takes his dog to the park. (*three times a week*)

______

6 We play computer games on Saturdays. (*always*)

______

7 We meet up for coffee on Sunday. (*usually*)

______

➤ Go back to page 5.

1.3 Indefinite pronouns

A Choose the correct option.

1 I need *something's* / *somebody's* help.
2 I want to go *somewhere* / *something* new.
3 There is *nobody* / *nothing* I can do.
4 We don't need *everything* / *anything* else.
5 We go *everywhere* / *anywhere* together.
6 *Someone* / *Anyone* broke the ice.
7 *No one* / *Someone* came to Vant's party.

B Complete the sentences with the correct indefinite pronouns.

1 Somebody/Someone left a comment.
2 ______ could get online – there was no internet connection.
3 Do you know ______ at this party?
4 I don't want to speak to you. I have ______ to say to you.
5 Did you write ______ on her Facebook page?
6 There is ______ unusual about this signature. It's strange!
7 They live ______ in Romania.

➤ Go back to page 7.

Grammar Hub

2.1 Adverbs of degree

almost	= *nearly*	She **almost** fell from the balcony.
completely	= 100%	This is a **completely** new idea.
extremely	= stronger than *very*	Life here is **extremely** expensive.
very		The city center is **very** lively at night.
so	= *very*	Living here is **so** convenient.
really	= *very*	This building is a **really** smart design.
fairly	= weaker than *very*	The town is **fairly** crowded on weekends.

- We use adverbs of degree to make something stronger or weaker.
- Adverbs of degree usually come **before** the adjective.
- We can also use *very*, *really*, *extremely* and *completely* before adjective + noun.

Be careful!

- We don't use *so* or *almost* before adjective + noun.
  It's so noisy. NOT ~~*It's a so noisy area.*~~
- We can also use adverbs of degree before adverbs.
  The pollution problem is improving ***very*** *slowly.*
- We can also use adverbs of degree before verbs.
- When a verb has an auxiliary verb (*have*, *be*, *do*), we usually put the adverb between the auxiliary verb and the main verb.

2.2 Simple present and present progressive

	Positive	Negative
I/you/we/they	**They love** their house.	**I don't live** in a big city.
he/she/it	**She loves** her family.	**He doesn't cook** every evening.

	Positive	Negative
I	**I'm studying** right now.	**I'm not studying** right now.
he/she/it	**She's living** with her parents.	**She isn't living** with her parents.
you/we/they	**We're moving** to the city.	**We aren't moving** to the city.

Question	Positive short answer	Negative short answer
Does he love cooking?	Yes, **he does**.	No, **he doesn't**.
Are they working?	Yes, **they are**.	No, **they aren't**.

- We use the simple present to talk about routines and things which are always or generally true.
- We use the present progressive to talk about temporary actions happening now or around now.
- We also use the present progressive to talk about trends.

2.3 Simple past – regular and irregular verbs

Subject	Positive	Negative
I/you/he/she/it/we/they	**He talked** to Jim yesterday.	**He didn't talk** to Jim yesterday.

Question	Positive short answer	Negative short answer
Did you talk to Jim yesterday?	Yes, **I did**.	No, **I didn't**.

- We use the simple past to talk about finished actions in the past.
- We usually use the time phrases *yesterday*, *an hour ago*, *on Monday*, *in 2015*, etc. with the simple past.

	Infinitive	Simple past positive
Add *-ed*.	ask	asked
Add *-d* after verbs ending *-e*.	decide	decided
Add *-ed* after verbs ending in a vowel + *-y*.	play	played
Change *-y* after a consonant to *-ied*.	study	studied
For verbs ending in a vowel and a consonant, double the consonant before adding *-ed*.	stop	stopped

2.1 Adverbs of degree

A Put the words in order to make sentences.

1 have / they / completely / new / a / designed / building / apartment
They have designed a completely new apartment building.

2 this / extremely / area / expensive / an / is
______

3 is / park / on / Sundays / crowded / so / the
______

4 cars / move / slowly / city / the / in / very
______

5 polluted / is / in / it / places / some / fairly
______

6 ready / am / move / to / I / almost
______

7 is / really / there / beautiful / park / a / here / near
______

B Choose the correct option.

1 I'm (*so*) / ***almost*** happy to be living in London!
2 Cleaning up the city is ***almost*** / ***extremely*** expensive.
3 Our new apartment is ***almost*** / ***really*** nice. I love it!
4 Architects used a ***so*** / ***completely*** new design.
5 In the summer, it gets ***extremely*** / ***completely*** hot here.
6 It is ***almost*** / ***very*** impossible to get to know everyone in your neighborhood.
7 My last house was ***fairly a*** / ***fairly*** big, but I didn't have enough space.

➤ Go back to page 13.

2.2 Simple present and present progressive

A Correct the mistakes in each sentence. Use contractions where possible.

1 ~~We be~~ *We're* living in Rome right now.
2 I stay at my parents' house this week.
3 She's liking doing the laundry very much.
4 They're usually helping with the housework on Sundays.
5 Paul's doing the cooking most of the time.
6 We both look for a permanent job right now.

B Complete the sentences with the correct form of the verb in parentheses. Use contractions where possible.

1 I *'m studying* (*study*) French history this year.
2 My mom still ______ (*do*) all my laundry.
3 I ______ (*not / need*) you to help me look for a new place.
4 What ______ (*you / argue*) about now?
5 They ______ (*save*) money to buy a house.
6 She ______ (*not / always / cook*) for herself.
7 He ______ (*talk*) to his cousin right now.

➤ Go back to page 15.

2.3 Simple past – regular and irregular verbs

A Put the verbs into the simple past. Use contractions where possible.

1 They (*go*) to Amsterdam yesterday. *went*
2 She (*not / visit*) her parents on the weekend. ______
3 I (*buy*) a new laptop. ______
4 (*you / bring*) your bag with you? ______
5 Dan (*take*) the train to work this morning. ______
6 I (*not / leave*) work until 10 last night. ______
7 We (*not / be*) worried when we took our exams. ______

B Complete the conversation with the simple past form of the verbs.

Will: (1) ______ (*you / enjoy*) your childhood?

Rebecca: Yes, my friends and I (2) ______ (*go*) to the movie theater a lot, and we played on our bikes. What sort of things (3) ______ (*you / do*)?

Will: I (4) ______ (*not / have*) a good time. My school (5) ______ (*be*) terrible. I (6) ______ (*take*) my exams three times before I passed.

Rebecca: Oh dear! So you didn't have much free time, I imagine.

Will: Exactly!

➤ Go back to page 17.

Grammar Hub

3.1 *all / some / most / no / none*

- We use *all*, *some*, *most* and *no* before nouns.

  *Give him **all** the money.*
  *There are **no** taxis.*

- We can use *all*, *some*, *most* and *none* with *of* + pronoun or *the/this/that/these/those*.

  *I've stayed in many hotels and I liked **most of** them.*
  *I like **all of** the Greek islands.*
  Some of her trips were by bus.
  None of the countries were in Africa.

- With *all*, we don't have to use *of* before a pronoun + noun or *the/this/that/these/those*.

  *Did you spend **all your** money? OR Did you spend **all of** your money?*

- With *all*, we must use *of* before a pronoun without a noun.

  *Did you spend **all of it**? NOT ~~Did you spend all it?~~*

- We cannot use *no* with *of* + pronoun or *the/this/that/these/those*.

  None of us want to leave. NOT ~~No of us want to leave.~~

3.2 Past progressive and simple past

	Positive	Negative
I/you/he/she/it/we/they	**They traveled** by train all night.	We **didn't go** by ferry.

Question	Positive short answer	Negative short answer
Did they enjoy the vacation?	Yes, **they did**.	No, **they didn't**.

- We use the simple past to talk about finished actions or situations, and things that happened one after another.
- See Grammar Reference 2.3 for more information about the simple past.

	Positive	Negative
I/he/she/it	**He was riding** the bus when his phone rang.	**She wasn't biking** to work when the rain started.
you/we/they	**They were sleeping** when I arrived.	**We weren't driving** when the car crashed.

Question	Positive short answer	Negative short answer
Was it snowing outside?	Yes, **it was**.	No, **it wasn't**.

- We use the past progressive for actions or situations that were unfinished at a past time.
- The past progressive describes a longer action and the simple past describes a shorter action.

  *They **were sailing** (=long action) from Portsmouth to Caen when the storm **hit** (=short action).*

- We use *when/while* before the past progressive to describe an action that was in progress when something else happened.

3.3 Verb + *-ing* and *to* + base form

- After some verbs (e.g. *agree*), we use *to* + base form.
- After some verbs (e.g. *enjoy*), we use *-ing*.
- After some verbs (e.g. *hate*), we can use either *to* + base form or *-ing*.

Verb	+ *to* + base form
can't afford	I **can't afford to buy** a new car.
hope	They **hope to meet** again soon.
learn	When did you **learn to drive**?
would like	We **would like to travel** the world.
would prefer	He **would prefer to go** to France.
Other verbs: agree / choose / decide / expect / manage / need / plan / refuse / seem / want	They **decided to go** by plane.

Verb	+ *-ing*
consider	She **considered saying** yes.
enjoy	We **enjoy reading** guide books.
avoid	He **avoided getting** wet on his trip.
spend time	Tina **spent time researching** the Andes.
Other verbs: advise / allow / begin / can't help / continue / finish / keep / mind / regret / stand	I **keep making** mistakes.

Verb	+ *to* + base form or *-ing*
hate	I **hate driving** in bad weather. OR I **hate to drive** in bad weather.
love	We **love visiting** Italy. OR We **love to visit** Italy.
prefer	I **prefer staying** in a hotel. OR I **prefer to stay** in a hotel.
like	They **like going** surfing. OR They **like to go** surfing.
Other verbs: begin / start	It **started to rain**. OR It **started raining**.

3.1 *all / some / most / no / none*

A Put the words in order to make sentences.

1 his / none / journeys / were / by / of / train

None of his journeys were by train.

2 dry / the / of / some / were / seats

____

3 all / the / unhappy / passengers / were

____

4 trip / us / none / wanted / end / of / to / the

____

5 kinds / most / don't / I / like / of / resorts / beach

____

6 have / money / no / left / wallets / our / we / in

____

7 Dilly / problems / airport / some / had / also / the / in

____

B Choose the correct option.

1 *No / None* of the tourists were paying attention.

2 All of *the people / people* were yelling.

3 Most *of taxis / taxis* in London are black.

4 I met *some of / some* nice people on my vacation.

5 How was your vacation? Did you enjoy *all / all of* it?

6 *No / None* visitors can go in this area.

➤ Go back to page 22.

3.2 Past progressive and simple past

A Correct the mistakes in each sentence.

1 We were living in London when the London Eye ~~was opening~~. *opened*

2 Jan was having an accident while she was sailing in the Pacific.

3 While they asking for directions, I looked at a guide book.

4 She traveled through China when she first met Clive.

5 The pilot was landing the plane when the crash was happening.

6 When the ferry crossed the ocean, we saw some dolphins.

7 She swam in the lake when something was biting her leg.

B Match to make sentences.

1	We were sailing around the island	a	I dropped my phone.
2	While I was taking photographs,	b	while she was lying by the pool.
3	They were not paying attention	c	while he was biking across Italy.
4	Someone stole her bag	d	while it was taking off.
5	He met Rob	e	when they got on the wrong bus.
6	Some birds hit the plane	f	when I started to feel sick.

➤ Go back to page 25.

3.3 Verb + *-ing* and *to* + base form

A Choose the correct option.

1 Avoid *to book / booking* a room at this hotel.

2 Consider *to write / writing* your own travel blog.

3 Refuse *to take / taking* no for an answer.

4 Spend time *to try / trying* different foods.

5 Learn *to enjoy / enjoying* life.

6 Don't agree *to get / getting* in the car with a stranger.

B Complete the text messages with the correct forms of the verbs.

Fay: I would like (**1**) ______________ (*stay*) somewhere fun for a weekend trip. Any ideas?

Joy: What about a campsite?

Fay: I can't stand (**2**) ______________ (*sleep*) outdoors. Maybe a hostel or a guest house?

Joy: I don't mind (**3**) ______________ (*go*) to either. Which would you prefer?

Fay: I'd prefer (**4**) ______________ (*stay*) at a hostel. Sound OK?

Joy: Yes, I enjoy (**5**) ______________ (*meet*) new people.

Fay: Great! I can't afford (**6**) ______________ (*spend*) much money.

Joy: Then a hostel is a good choice – they usually have low prices.

➤ Go back to page 27.

Grammar Hub

4.1 *be going to* + base form and present progressive for the future

	Positive	Negative
I	**I'm going to meet** my friends.	**I'm not going to have** a night out.
he/she/it	**He's going to play** billiards.	**She isn't going to relax** at home.
you/we/they	**They're going to spend** the evening at home.	**We aren't going to see** a play on the weekend.

Question	Positive short answer	Negative short answer
Is he going to hang out with us?	Yes, **he is**.	No, **he isn't**.
Are they going to have a party to celebrate?	Yes, **they are**.	No, **they aren't**.

- We use *be going to* to talk about intentions.

	Positive	Negative
I	**I'm meeting** Steff at 6.	**I'm not having** dinner with Steve tonight.
he/she/it	**She's going** to the movies on Saturday.	**She isn't visiting** her grandparents this weekend.
you/we/they	**We're visiting** Tina tomorrow.	**We aren't playing** in the concert next week.

Question	Positive short answer	Negative short answer
Am I meeting you at 8?	Yes, **you are**.	No, **you aren't**.
Are you watching a movie tonight?	Yes, **we are**.	No, **we aren't**.

- We use the present progressive to talk about arrangements in the future.

Be careful!

- We don't use the present progressive for intentions.

I'm going to open my own restaurant when I'm older. NOT ~~*I'm opening my own restaurant when I'm older.*~~

4.2 Making predictions

	Positive	Negative
I/you/he/she/it/we/they	**He will go** on a virtual date.	**It won't be** very romantic.
	They may/might fall in love.	**It may/might not be** easy to meet people.

Question	Positive short answer	Negative short answer
Will they go out for dinner?	Yes, **they will**.	No, **they won't**.

- We use *will*, *may* and *might* to make predictions about the future. We use *will* when we are certain. We use *may* or *might* when we are less certain. There is little difference in meaning between *may* and *might*.

- Because *will*, *may* and *might* are modals, they only have one form.

She might bring her VR headset. NOT ~~*She mights bring her VR headset.*~~

- We use adverbs of probability with *will* to make predictions more or less certain.

100% *We'll **definitely/certainly** need to bring a warm blanket.*
75% *She'll **probably** stay at home with her family.*
50% ***Maybe** they'll go on vacation to Denmark.*
25% *I **probably** won't cook a meal.*
0% *You **definitely** won't forget the experience.*

Be careful!

- *Maybe* goes at the beginning of the sentence.

Maybe you'll play board games. NOT ~~*You'll maybe play board games.*~~

4.3 Subject and object questions

- We ask subject questions when we don't know what/who/which/whose something (or someone) is.

What is hygge?

- We ask object questions when we want to know more information about something (or someone).

How do you pronounce hygge?

- Subject questions don't include an auxiliary verb. Object questions do.

Subject question: Whose blanket is this?
*Object question: Which restaurant **did** you go to?*

- With subject questions, we don't change the word order in the answer.

Who is your best friend? Friya is my best friend.

- In object questions, the question word is the object of the sentence.

***What** do you do to relax? I play **computer games** to relax.*

4.1 *be going to* + base form and present progressive for the future

A Correct the mistakes in each sentence.

1. I'm going to ~~introducing~~ *introduce* you to my friends.
2. She going to the theater with Alice tonight.
3. We meet Pamela at 4 pm this afternoon.
4. They going to cook pizza for everyone.
5. She's going buy a cake for his birthday.
6. What time we meeting for lunch?

B Put the words in order to make sentences.

1. to / invite / my colleagues / I'm / to the party / going / all
   I'm going to invite all my colleagues to the party.
2. to / I / going / tonight / think / at home / I'm / stay
   ______
3. are / that new sushi place / to / Karl and Inge / going / try
   ______
4. sister / seeing / you / again / when / are / your / ?
   ______
5. on Friday night / having / Tom's / a birthday party
   ______
6. at five o'clock / meeting / we're / in the central square
   ______

➤ Go back to page 33.

4.2 Making predictions

A Choose the correct option.

1. I *definitely* / *maybe* won't go to the concert because it's raining.
2. *Maybe you will* / *You maybe will* be home early on Friday.
3. They *will* / *might* definitely go sailing tonight.
4. Robots *might* / *definitely* won't understand human feelings in the future. I don't believe that's possible.
5. I *may* / *will* not have enough money for the tickets. Let's see how much they are.
6. We probably *might not* / *won't* have the party next week.
7. I'll definitely *going* / *go* to college when I leave high school.

B Make sentences with *will* or *might*.

1. Robots ______ (*definitely / do*) all the work in the future.
2. We ______ (*control*) computers with our minds in the future. It's possible.
3. It ______ (*not / be*) a good idea to sell my car. I need to think about it.
4. They ______ (*probably / not / go*) to the party.
5. I don't think robots ______ (*have*) feelings.
6. It ______ (*not / cost*) more than 20 dollars. That's for sure.

➤ Go back to page 35.

4.3 Subject and object questions

A Complete the sentences with the question words in the box. Then select the correct question type: subject (S) or object (O).

how	what	when	where	who	why

1. ______ is going on the trip to Denmark? S / O
2. ______ do you leave for Copenhagen? S / O
3. ______ is your favorite board game? S / O
4. ______ do you want to meet? S / O
5. ______ do you say 'hello' in French? S / O
6. ______ is our English class canceled? S / O

B Put the words in order to make questions. Then match the answers (a–f).

1. you / have / do / when / classes / English
   When do you have English classes? *f*
2. favorite / place / where / your / relaxing / is / for
   ______ __
3. does / do / she / free / time / what / her / in
   ______ __
4. feeling / Sara / is / how / driving test / about / the
   ______ __
5. they / for / when / leaving / are / Bucharest
   ______ __
6. best / the / is / who / cook / the / in / family
   ______ __

a. the bathtub
b. worried
c. next weekend
d. Fred
e. She goes to the gym.
f. on Thursdays

➤ Go back to page 37.

Grammar Hub

5.1 *can, could, be able to*

- We use *can* to talk about general possibility and ability in the present.

  I can choose when I work.
  They can't come to the meeting.
  Can I speak to you for a minute? Yes, you can. / No, you can't.
- We use *could* to talk about general possibility and ability in the past.

  She could work shifts when she was younger.
  They couldn't come to the meeting last Saturday.
  Could you take long vacations in your last job? Yes, I could. / No, I couldn't.
- We use *be able to* to talk about possibility and ability in the present, usually at a particular time or for a particular reason.

  I'm able to work with different people.
  He isn't able to work late tonight.
  Are they able to work nights? Yes, they are. / No, they aren't.
- We use *be able to* directly after another verb because *can* has no *-ing* or *to* + base form.

  I like being able to work nights. NOT ~~*I like can work nights.*~~
- We use *was/were able to* to talk about possibility and ability in the past, usually at a particular time or for a particular reason.

  She was able to find a new job.
  They weren't able to get the bus to work.
  Was he able to find the office? Yes, he was. / No, he wasn't.

5.2 Obligation, necessity and permission: *must, have to* and *can*

	Positive	Negative
I/you/he/she/it/we/they	**You can wear** casual clothes in the office. **You must get** to work before 9 am.	**You can't wear** jewelry. **You must not be** late.
I/you/we/they	**You have to get** to work before 9 am.	**They don't have to use** English at work.
he/she/it	**He has to get** to work before 9 am.	**She doesn't have to work** on Sundays.

Question	Positive short answer	Negative short answer
Can she wear earrings?	Yes, **she can**.	No, **she can't**.
Do we have to wear a tie?	Yes, **you do**.	No, **you don't**.
Does he have to have special training?	Yes, **he does**.	No, **he doesn't**.

- We use *can* for something that is allowed.
- We use *can't* for something that is not allowed.
- We use *must* and *have to* for something that is necessary or a rule.

Be careful!

- *Must not* has a different meaning to *don't have to*.

  must not = not allowed

  *You **must not** wear sportswear in the office.*

  must not = modal of deduction (in American English but NOT in British English)

  *They **must not** be at home. The car is gone.*

  don't have to = not necessary (but possible)

  *You **don't have to** wear dress clothes to work, but you can if you want.*
- In questions, we usually use *have to* and not *must*.

  *Do you **have to** wear boots?* NOT ~~*Must you wear boots?*~~

5.3 Present perfect with *for* and *since*

	Positive	Negative
I/you/we/they	**I've worked** here for 12 years.	**They haven't called** since last week.
he/she/it	**She's worked** in telemarketing since 2017.	**She hasn't checked** her messages for two days.

Question	Positive short answer	Negative short answer
Have you worked in a restaurant before?	Yes, **I have**.	No, **I haven't**.
Has he finished the project?	Yes, **he has**.	No, **he hasn't**.

- We use the present perfect to talk about actions and situations that started in the past but are unfinished and so continue until the present time.

  *I **have worked** here **for** three weeks. (= and I am still working here now)*
- We use *for* to show the amount of time, and *since* to show when the action or situation started.

  *She has been at this company **since** January.*
  *She has been at this company **for** six months.*
- We use *How long* plus the present perfect to ask about the length of time until the present.

  ***How long** has Maria **worked** there?*
- We also use the present perfect to talk about things that happened in the past at an unspecified time and our experiences up to now.

  I've done a lot of different jobs.

Be careful!

- The verb *go* has two past participles: *been* and *gone*.
- We use *been* when someone has gone somewhere and come back.

  Bill has been to a lot of job interviews.
- We use *gone* when someone has gone somewhere and not come back yet.

  Jeff has gone for an interview and he'll be back later.

5.1 *can, could, be able to*

A Complete the sentences with the words in the box.

able can (x2) can't could to were

1 As a manager, you ___can___ have a company car!
2 I __________ do this. Can you help me?
3 She's not __________ to work on Saturday.
4 __________ you work the night shift tomorrow?
5 We __________ able to get a lot of work done yesterday.
6 At my last job, I __________ start late on Fridays.
7 Brenda's self-employed so she's able __________ choose when she works.

B Put the words in order to make sentences.

1 hate / not / make / decisions / I / being / to / able
___I hate not being able to make decisions.___
2 wants / able / she / buy / to / house / be / to / a
____
3 last / in / finish / job / my / could / at / four / I
____
4 wants / able / to / she / take / be / long / vacation / a / to
____
5 training / he / do / the / can't / because / involves / special / job / it
____
6 they / being / like / from / work / able / home / to
____

➤ Go back to page 43.

5.2 Obligation, necessity and permission: *must, have to* and *can*

A Choose the correct option.

1 You *can't* / *can* do this job unless you have training.
2 You *must not* / *don't have to* do this work today. Next week's fine.
3 We *can* / *must* wear casual clothes on a Monday. It's our choice.
4 You *can* / *have to* believe in your idea for it to be a success.
5 Simon *must not* / *doesn't have to* be rude to the manager. He'll lose his job!
6 I *can* / *don't have to* take the bus. It's easy to walk there.
7 Everyone *can* / *must* start work at 9. It's a rule.

B Complete the text messages with the words in the box.

can can't don't have to has to have to

Hannah: (**1**) __________ you meet me and Lily for coffee after work – at five thirty?

Fatima: No, I (**2**) __________. We (**3**) __________ work late today, remember?

Hannah: Oh, yeah. Well, I (**4**) __________ work late because I did all my work this morning. Have you asked Lily?

Fatima: She (**5**) __________ stay too. She told me this morning.

Hannah: OK. Another time then.

➤ Go back to page 45.

5.3 Present perfect with *for* and *since*

A Choose the correct option.

1 I have wanted to work there *for* / *since* a long time.
2 I have worked here *for* / *since* 2014.
3 We haven't had a day off *for* / *since* a long time.
4 They've worked in recruitment *for* / *since* the last 10 years.
5 She hasn't spoken to the manager *for* / *since* months.
6 Giles hasn't worked *for* / *since* he lost his job in accounts.
7 Things have changed *for* / *since* we did our research.

B Make sentences with the present perfect.

1 she / do / a lot of charity work
___She's done a lot of charity work.___
2 they / be / in your office / for an hour
____
3 you / change / your appointment / three times
____
4 we / not have / a pay raise / for a while
____
5 How long / she / be / the owner of the company / ?
____

➤ Go back to page 47.

6.1 Quantifiers *too* and *enough*

- We use *too* + adjective or adverb, *too much* and *too many* to mean more than the right amount.

*I am **too tired**.*

*You drink **too much** cola and you eat **too many** candies.*

Be careful!

- We use *too many* with countable nouns.

*They buy **too many** snacks.*

- We use *too much* with uncountable nouns.

*We eat **too much** sugar.*

- We use *enough* + noun to mean the right amount.

*We have **enough** drinks for everyone.*

- We use *not enough* + noun to mean less than the right amount.

*She **doesn't have enough** time to cook.*

Be careful!

- When we use *too* and *enough* with adjectives or adverbs, we put *too* **before** the adjective or adverb and *enough* **after** the adjective or adverb.

*I feel **too sick** to have dinner.*

*I don't feel **well enough** to have dinner.*

*You exercise **too hard**.*

*You don't exercise **hard enough**.*

6.2 *-ing* forms

- We use the present participle *-ing* form to talk about things that are happening now or around now and that are not finished. This is the present progressive.

*You're **doing** really well at yoga.*

- We use the *-ing* form as an adjective to describe a noun.

*He has developed a **growing** interest in Nordic walking.*

- We use the *-ing* form as a gerund to make a noun.

*They like **working out** at the gym twice a week.*

6.3 Present perfect with *just*, *already* and *yet*

	Positive	Negative
I/you/we/they	**I've** just **seen** the doctor.	**I haven't seen** the doctor yet.
he/she/it	**She's left** the hospital already.	**He hasn't gone** to the gym yet.

Question	Positive short answer	Negative short answer
Have you taken your painkillers yet?	Yes, **I have**.	No, **I haven't**.
Has the nurse just **given** you some medicine?	Yes, **he has**.	No, **he hasn't**.

- We use the present perfect with *just* in positive statements to say that something happened very recently.

*I have **just** passed my fitness test.*

- We use the present perfect with *already* in positive statements to say that something happened before now, or earlier than expected.

*We have been to the grocery store twice today **already**.*

- We use the present perfect with *yet* in negative statements to say that something hasn't happened, but it still might.

*You haven't finished your vegetables **yet**.*

- We use the present perfect with *yet* in questions to ask if something has happened.

*Have you cleared the dinner table **yet**?*

Be careful!

- *Just* goes before the past participle.

*I've **just** eaten some fruit.* NOT ~~*I've eaten some fruit just.*~~

- *Yet* goes at the end of the sentence.

*Have you gone vegetarian **yet**?* NOT ~~*Have you yet gone vegetarian?*~~

- In American English, *already* usually goes at the end of the sentence. In British English, *already* goes before the past participle.

*I've stopped eating meat **already**.* OR *I've **already** stopped eating meat.*

- See Grammar Reference 5.3 for more information about the present perfect.

6.1 Quantifiers *too* and *enough*

A Choose the correct option.

1 Don't eat too *much* / *many* eggs.
2 I am *enough* / *too* tired to jog.
3 Make sure you are getting *enough* / *too much* sleep.
4 You don't drink *enough* / *too much* water.
5 I have eaten too *many* / *much* candy.
6 The gym closes *too* / *enough* early.
7 We don't have *enough* / *too much* food in the fridge.

B Match to make sentences.

1 We have too ___ a enough exercise.
2 You don't do ___ b sick for soccer practice.
3 We don't have ___ c people in this yoga class.
4 There are too many ___ d enough milk.
5 She has too much ___ e many cups on the table.
6 He's too ___ f energy to sit still.

➤ Go back to page 53.

6.2 *-ing* forms

A Correct the mistakes in each sentence.

1 We both enjoy ~~go~~ going for walks.
2 To jog is my favorite form of exercise.
3 I'm watch a good TV show about superfoods.
4 She doesn't like swim in the ocean.
5 Recently, there has been an increase number of accidents in the home.
6 My nextdoor neighbor isn't to do very well right now.
7 A rise number of people can't afford to buy medicine.

B Put the words in order to make sentences. Then choose gerund (*G*), adjective (*A*) or present participle (*PP*) for the words in **bold**.

1 doesn't / **being** / her / on / like / she / own — *G* / *A* / *PP*
She doesn't like being on her own.
2 love / doctor / **visiting** / we / family / our — *G* / *A* / *PP*
___
3 now / **growing** / in / there / is / interest / a / pilates — *G* / *A* / *PP*
___
4 **studying** / food / we're / health / in / class / groups — *G* / *A* / *PP*
___
5 my / **cooking** / free time / activity / favorite / is — *G* / *A* / *PP*
___
6 now / people / vitamins / of / taking / **increasing** / are / numbers — *G* / *A* / *PP*
___

➤ Go back to page 55.

6.3 Present perfect with *just*, *already* and *yet*

A Write *just*, *already* or *yet*.

1 Have you had anything to eat ___?
2 He hasn't asked her to work out with him ___.
3 I've run two marathons this year ___.
4 She's ___ finished her workout – she's showering now.
5 It's only 11 a.m., but Jack's eaten his lunch ___.
6 **A:** Who was on the phone?
B: Frida. She's ___ returned home from the hospital.

B Make sentences with the present perfect and *just*, *already* and *yet*.

1 you / see / your exam results / ?
Have you seen your exam results yet?
2 they / lose / 5 pounds / from their diet
___
3 I / have / a phone call / from the nurse
___
4 we / not use / our new oven
___
5 she / take / her medicine / today
___
6 you / buy / the food / for tonight / ?
___
7 I / see / Pamela / in the grocery store
___

➤ Go back to page 57.

1.1 People

A SPEAK Work in pairs. Look at the pictures. Describe the people and their relationships. Use the words in the box to help you.

children colleagues couple friends grandparents parents relatives strangers students teacher

B Choose the correct words to complete the sentences.

1 Sally and Nicole are good ***friends*** / ***strangers*** and they go to the same college.
2 Jamal is a photography ***colleague*** / ***teacher***. He knows a lot about cameras.
3 Every weekend, I go to stay at my ***grandparents'*** / ***couple's*** house.
4 I never know what to say to ***strangers*** / ***parents*** when I meet them for the first time.
5 Janelle and Carla are ***colleagues*** / ***students***, and they work together in the office very well.
6 All of my ***relatives*** / ***teachers*** live in the same town – we're a very close family.

➤ Go back to page 3.

1.2 Types of people

A Match the descriptions (1–10) with the types of people in **bold** in *Three of the best*.

1 a person who likes animals _animal lover_
2 a woman who has three children ________
3 a person who is very interested in food ________
4 a person who enjoys seeing other places ________
5 a person who watches or takes part in sports ________
6 a person who plays computer games ________
7 a person who enjoys spending time with others ________
8 a person who loves reading ________
9 a person who writes online regularly ________
10 a person who listens to music regularly ________

B Complete the sentences with the words in the box.

coffee dog father positive soccer

1 I'm a ________ owner. I take it for a walk twice a day.
2 I'm a big ________ drinker. Cappuccino is my favorite, but I also like espresso.
3 I'm a ________ of two. My wife and I have two daughters.
4 I'm a ________ person. I try not to worry or complain.
5 I'm a ________ fan. My favorite team is Manchester United.

➤ Go back to page 4.

2.3 Life events

Match the life events (1–10) with the pictures (a–j).

1 have a baby / children
2 go to college
3 get a job
4 get married
5 leave home
6 fall in love
7 get your own place
8 retire
9 learn to swim
10 leave school

➤ Go back to page 17.

3.3 Accommodations and amenities

A Label the pictures with the words in the box. Which types of accommodations have you stayed in?

apartment beach resort campsite chalet cruise ship five-star hotel guest house hostel

1 ______________

2 ______________

3 ______________

4 ______________

5 ______________

6 ______________

7 ______________

8 ______________

B SPEAK Work in pairs. What do the words in **bold** mean? Explain them. Then decide who would say each sentence. Write guest (*G*) or receptionist (*R*).

1 The **front desk** is open 24 hours. Just dial nine on the phone in your room.
2 We don't have any **double** or **twin rooms** for tonight, I'm afraid, but there are two **single rooms** available.
3 I understand the **dorms** in the hostel are non-smoking, but can I smoke on the **balcony**?
4 All our rooms have **safes** for your valuables, quiet **air conditioners** and beautiful **ocean views**.
5 Hello, is that **room service**? I'd like to order some food, please. It's room 442.
6 If you'd like to exercise or have a massage, our **gym**, pool and **spa** are on the fourth floor.
7 We're **checking out** tomorrow and we'd like to book an **airport transfer** for 10 am, please.
8 You have booked a **self-service apartment**, but there is a restaurant by the pool if you'd like to eat there.

➤ Go back to page 27.

4.2 Suffixes

A Complete the diagrams with the verbs in the box. Check your answers in the *Macmillan English Dictionary*.

agree ~~develop~~ ~~discuss~~ improve invent predict

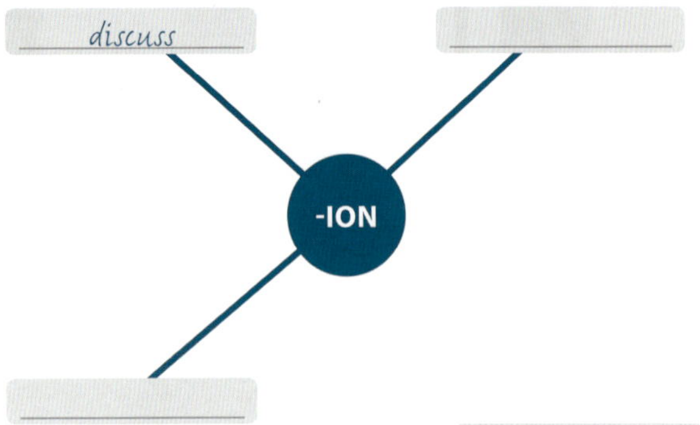

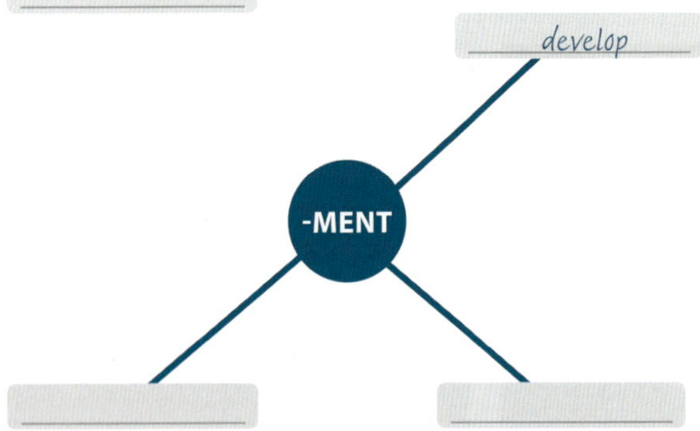

B Complete the diagrams with the adjectives in the box. You need to change the spelling in some of the words when you add a suffix. Which ones? Check your answers in the *Macmillan English Dictionary*.

~~able~~ active ~~happy~~ kind possible sad

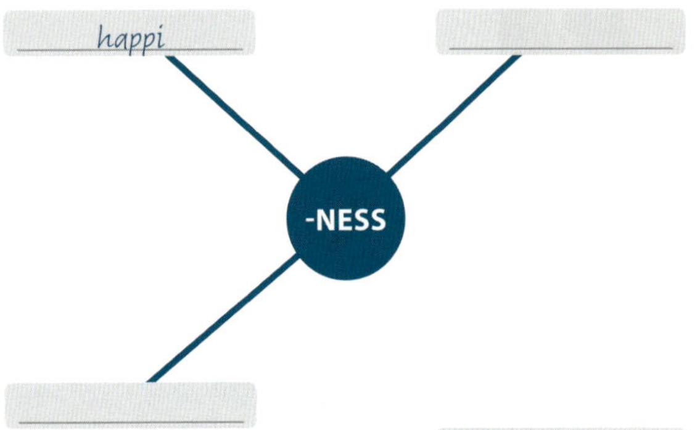

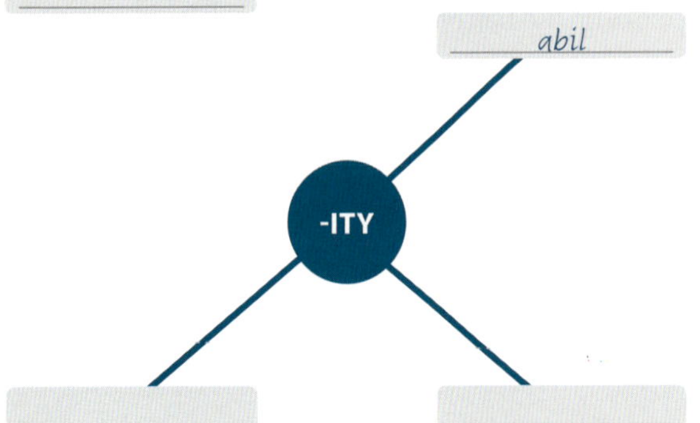

➤ Go back to page 35.

4.3 Relaxing

A Complete the blanks in blue in the survey with the words in the box. Read *Make yourself at home* on page 36 again to help you.

a good book board games by the fire friends or family get together homemade food hot bath quiet night relaxed atmosphere simple things some candles some time out

How *hygge* is your lifestyle?

1 It's a rainy Sunday afternoon. Do you prefer to …

a go to a shopping center and spend some money?
b order delivery food and switch on the game console?
c sit down with [1]_______________ and read all afternoon under a cozy blanket?

2 How would you rather celebrate your birthday?

a Go out with friends and stay out until late.
b Meet friends in the [2]_______________ of a café or restaurant and have a nice meal.
c Have [3]_______________ over to eat [4]_______________ and play [5]_______________.

3 What makes you happiest?

a Money, shopping, vacations, etc.
b A chance to [6]_______________ with family and friends.
c The [7]_______________ in life, like a [8]_______________ in or a long walk in the country.

4 It's Friday night and your workweek is over. Would you rather …

a go out with your colleagues?
b go home, watch TV and have an early night?
c go home, have a nice, [9]_______________ and then sit [10]_______________ and dry off?

5 How do you create the perfect atmosphere at home?

a Turn on the lights, turn up the music and dance around the living room.
b Close the curtains, turn on the TV and lie on the couch.
c Light [11]_______________, play some soft music and take [12]_______________ to relax.

Finished? Work out your score: a = 0, b = 1, c = 2

B SPEAK Work in pairs. Ask and answer the questions in Exercise A. Make a note of your partner's answers. Go to the **Communication Hub** on **page XXIII** and check your scores. Who has more *hygge* in their lives?

➤ Go back to page 37.

5.3 *work* + preposition

A Complete the diagram with the words in the box.

a design firm | a hospital | accounts | Volkswagen

work

+ *at/for* + a named company, for example, 1 ______________

+ *for* + type of company, for example, 2 ______________

+ *in* + area of business or department, for example, 3 ______________

+ *at/in* + place, for example, 4 ______________

B Write the correct prepositions to complete the sentences.

1 He works ________ Base One IT Services.
2 We work ________ a law firm.
3 They work ________ a restaurant.
4 She works ________ a telemarketing company.
5 He works ________ the IT department.
6 They work ________ Human Resources.

➤ Go back to page 47.

6.2 Exercise

A Label the pictures of sports and activities with the words in the box.

biking | field hockey | jogging | marathon running | Nordic walking | racquetball | working out at the gym | yoga

B Complete the instructions with the correct form of the verbs in the box. You will need to use some of the verbs more than once.

burn | do | go | lose | play | run | stay | ~~work out~~

Find someone who …

1 hates *working out* at the gym.
2 can give a tip on how to ______________ weight in a healthy way.
3 ______________ jogging or running regularly.
4 knows someone who has ______________ a marathon, a half-marathon or a 10 km race.
5 knows how to ______________ racquetball.
6 ______________ in shape by walking or biking to school or work.
7 knows how many calories an average person ______________ in a day.
8 ______________ yoga or goes to an exercise class.
9 has a parent or grandparent who ______________ Nordic walking.
10 regularly ______________ a team sport such as field hockey or soccer when they were in school.

➤ Go back to page 54.

6.3 Food groups

A Write the food words in the box in the correct place.

avocado | banana | cod | lettuce | lobster | oats | rice | shrimp | tomato | tuna | wheat

Fruits and vegetables	Grains	Seafood

B Complete the lists with words from Exercise A.

1 Foods that are mostly used in salads: cucumber, ______________, ______________.
2 Foods that are used in breakfast cereals: nuts, ______________, ______________, ______________.
3 Examples of shellfish: crab, ______________, ______________.

C Complete the sentences with words from Exercise A.

1 I think I'll have a ______________ sandwich.
2 The ______________ is ground into flour, and this is the main ingredient of bread.
3 A prawn looks just like a ______________, but is smaller.
4 Sushi is made with raw fish, rice and sometimes ______________ and ______________.
5 I prefer white fish, like haddock and ______________.

➤ Go back to page 57.

3.3 Student A

The central three-star Hotel Rambla Park is 50 m from Barcelona's famous Las Ramblas walking street and close to some of its best stores, markets and restaurants. This attractive hotel has a good restaurant with room service and a small pool. All rooms are non-smoking and have air conditioners, free wi-fi and a TV. One-way airport transfers are available for 15 dollars per person. The front desk is open 24 hours.

Room type: Double or twin room (extra bed available) – 40 dollars per person, per night including breakfast. Single room: 60 dollars per night including breakfast.

Share Like Comment

➤ Go back to page 27.

3.3 Student C

The Olympic Apartments are close to Barcelona's beaches and have beautiful ocean views. The famous Las Ramblas walking street is a 20-minute walk away. The two- and three-bedroom with room service apartments are simple and clean. Guests can pay to use the gym and spa on the first floor. Stores, public transportation and restaurants are all very close. All apartments have a balcony and air conditioners. Wi-fi is available for an extra 5 dollars per day.

Room type: Two-bedroom with room service apartment – 100 dollars per night for up to four people.

➤ Go back to page 27.

5.1 Groups

Group A jobs: banker, nanny, professional soccer player, politician

Group B jobs: doctor, pilot, social worker, actor

Group C jobs: lawyer, nurse, soldier, teacher

➤ Go back to page 43.

4.2 Student B

Social media

Social media is everywhere and is a normal part of many people's lives. However, experts agree that the way we use social media will change in the future.

Ten years ago, people used social media to share messages. Then everyone got cameras on their phones and began sharing pictures and video. But if Mark Zuckerberg of Facebook is right, you and your friends will soon put on your VR (Virtual Reality) headsets and meet in amazing 3D virtual worlds. Zuckerberg and Facebook are spending a lot of money on developing VR social media.

With VR social media, it will be possible to meet your friends 'inside' pictures and videos. This means, for example, that you will be able to spend time together at the top of mountains or the bottom of oceans! It will also be possible to hang out in virtual versions of real clubs or museums, or just about anywhere in the world (or the universe) you can imagine.

There is still a lot of work to do on the technology, so you might have to wait a while before you can share your selfies from the far side of the moon! However, experts agree that VR is the future of social media.

Glossary

expert (n) someone who knows a lot about a particular subject
virtual (adj) almost the same as the real thing

➤ Go back to page 34

3.3 Student B

Gaudí House Hostel is a half-hour walk or ten-minute bus trip from the center of Barcelona and is perfect for travelers on a budget. The eight-person dorms (choose between male only, female only or mixed) are comfortable, the bathrooms are clean and the kitchen area has everything you need to cook for yourself. Guests can leave their valuables in the safe at the front desk. Wi-fi is available in the front desk area. (Note: air conditioning is not available in dorm rooms.)

Room type: Dorm bed 25 dollars per person, per night. (Add breakfast for only 5 dollars per person, per day!)

Share Like Comment

➤ Go back to page 27.

4.2 Student A

Work–life balance

Everybody loves long weekends, so why do they happen so rarely? When we have three full days off work, there is more time to relax and spend time with friends and family. The good news is that some people think it might not be long until *every* weekend is a long weekend.

Experts and business leaders predict that better technology will do more of our work for us. This will allow us to have shorter workweeks in the future. In fact, it is already beginning to happen. Carlos Slim, the famous Mexican telecoms billionaire, has introduced a shorter week for some of his older, more experienced employees. In Japan, companies such as car maker Toyota have found that working shorter hours leads to happier employees, and higher profits.

A better work–life balance won't be the only good thing about shorter workweeks. Offices will use less energy for lighting, computers and air conditioning. Also, there will be fewer car trips to work, which is better for the environment.

Glossary

expert (n) someone who knows a lot about a particular subject
profit (n) money you make by selling something or from your business

➤ Go back to page 34.

4.2 Student C

ROBOT RELATIONSHIPS

Meet Pepper, the world's friendliest robot. Pepper's Japanese makers say the cute little robot can understand 70–80 percent of conversations with a human. They even say Pepper can understand when someone is happy or sad. And this is just the beginning. Experts predict that in the future, humans will probably develop close relationships with robots.

Right now, most of the robots in Japan look like Pepper, but it definitely won't be long until robots look, sound and move like humans. Erica, a robot developed by Professor Hiroshi Ishiguro of Osaka University, can show basic feelings on her face and gives us a better idea of what is already possible.

Experts such as Ishiguro think that developments in technology might help scientists to make machines that really understand human feelings. This means your robot might be able to figure out if you are happy or sad and use this information to talk and behave like a friend. That could make it possible for robots to take care of people. Some experts even believe that one day it may be possible for robots to feel love.

Glossary

expert (n) someone who knows a lot about a particular subject

4.3 *Hygge* scores

What does your score mean?

7–10 points: Your lifestyle is already very *hygge*. Have you thought about moving to Denmark?!

4–6 points: Your lifestyle is fairly *hygge*, but you could still learn a thing or two from the Danes.

0–3 points: Your lifestyle is not *hygge* at all. Be kind to yourself and let some more *hygge* into your life!

➤ Go back to page XX.

3.2 Students A and B

Work in pairs. Look at the pictures and tell a story. Think about:

- what happened during the journey.
- what decisions the people made.
- how the people felt at the end of the journey.

➤ Go back to page 25.

3.2 Students C and D

Work in pairs. Look at the pictures to tell a story. Think about:

1 What happened during the journey?
2 What decisions did people make?
3 How did the people feel at the end of the journey?

➤ Go back to page 25.

W — checking your writing

Use it or lose it

Welcome. This is a blog for language learners written by … a language learner!
My favorite tip for people interested in learning languages is 'use it or lose it'. It means 'practice the language and you won't forget it'. I started this blog to practice my English. Would you like to practice your English? Send me a message in English and I'll reply. Twice a week, I'll post the most interesting messages on the blog.

About me

I'm Karolina. Tea drinker, [1]bloger and hard-working [2]langage learner. [3]I've 20 years old and I'm Polish. I study law in college, and English in my free time. I go to English classes [4]three times week and I practice for half an hour every day. I have to be [5]wel organized to get everything done! Of course, I'm [6]serious with learning, but I also really enjoy it.

My blog [7]aren't my only hobby. I'm a book lover and I'm also [8]interest in old black and white movies. I read and watch in Polish and English.

I'm a curious, sociable person and [9]I like talk to people who ask questions. I'm interested in creative types and I love meeting new people – especially other language learners (in the real world and online). I think that makes me a [10]person people. I hope you enjoy the blog. Remember … use it or lose it!

A Read the home page of Karolina's blog and answer the questions.

1 What is her blog about and who is it for?
2 How can you help Karolina?

B Work in pairs. Read the *About me* section of Karolina's blog. Then cover the blog and discuss what you remember about:

1 her work or studies
2 her likes and dislikes
3 the type of person she is

C Work in pairs. In Karolina's *About me* section there are ten mistakes with grammar, vocabulary and spelling. Correct them. Use the information in the box to help you.

Checking your writing

Follow these tips to help make your writing better.

- Always read your writing slowly and carefully before you finish.
- Try and find and correct any mistakes.
- Check your grammar.
- Check the vocabulary and spelling and be careful with any new language.

D Which colors are the different types of mistakes in Karolina's writing?

1 grammar mistakes ______
2 vocabulary mistakes ______
3 spelling mistakes ______

E Find and correct one mistake in each sentence. Then decide what type of mistake it is. Write grammar (*G*), vocabulary (*V*) or spelling (*S*).

1 I love to travell and I study tourism. ______ __
2 Why you did start this blog? ______ __
3 I try to learn a new word ever day. ______ __
4 I usually am online during the evenings. ______ __
5 I guess I'm an independant type. ______ __
6 I'm responsible with updating the website. ______ __
7 Are you want to know more about our group? ______ __
8 I've never write a blog before. ______ __

WRITING

A PLAN You are going to write an *About me* section for your own blog, website or social media page. Take notes about your work or studies, your likes and dislikes and the type of person you are.

B WRITE Use your notes and Writing Exercise A to help you write your blog. Then check your writing using the list below and the strategies in the Writing skills box.

- ☐ I have mentioned my work or studies.
- ☐ I have mentioned some of my likes and dislikes.
- ☐ I have described my personality and the type of person I am.
- ☐ I have checked my work for mistakes with grammar, vocabulary and spelling.

C REVIEW Work in groups. Read the group's profiles. Can you recommend any blogs, websites, magazines, books, TV shows or movies the people in your group might be interested in?

Write an email of complaint

W linking words

A Read Emma's email about a problem in her neighborhood. What is she complaining about?

To: Mr. Black
Re: Road safety complaint

Dear Mr. Black,

I'm writing to complain about the dangerous roads outside my apartment building.

My main complaint is that the roads are dangerous **because** there are no crosswalks **or** traffic lights outside my apartment building. This is a problem for a number of reasons.

First of all, the traffic is very fast on the main road **and** this makes crossing difficult for older people and mothers with young children. The second problem is that there is a popular children's play area across from the main road, **but** the children have no way to cross the road to use the play area. The last problem is that the grocery store parking lot entrance is on the corner of two busy roads, **so** it makes it more difficult to cross the road.

I would like to offer you two solutions for this problem. First of all, I think you should make a crosswalk on the busy road between the grocery store and the children's play area. I also think you need to make a second crosswalk across the main road from the apartment building to the play area. You could put traffic lights on this intersection to make it safe for children to use.

I hope you will make this dangerous road safer for the older people and children in our neighborhood.

I'm looking forward to hearing from you.

Sincerely yours,

Emma Lopez

B Read again and answer the questions.

1 How many problems and solutions does Emma mention?
2 Do you think Mr. Black will do what Emma wants him to do?
3 What tense does she use to begin and end her email?

C Look at the words in **bold** in Emma's email. Then complete the rules in the box with *and*, *but*, *or*, *so*, or *because*.

Linking words

We can join sentences and link ideas with *and*, *but*, *or*, *so* and *because*. This helps you to write longer and more interesting sentences.

We use 1 __________ to add more information.
We use 2 __________ to give contrasting information.
We use 3 __________ to give a negative alternative.
We use 4 __________ to give a result.
We use 5 __________ to explain why.

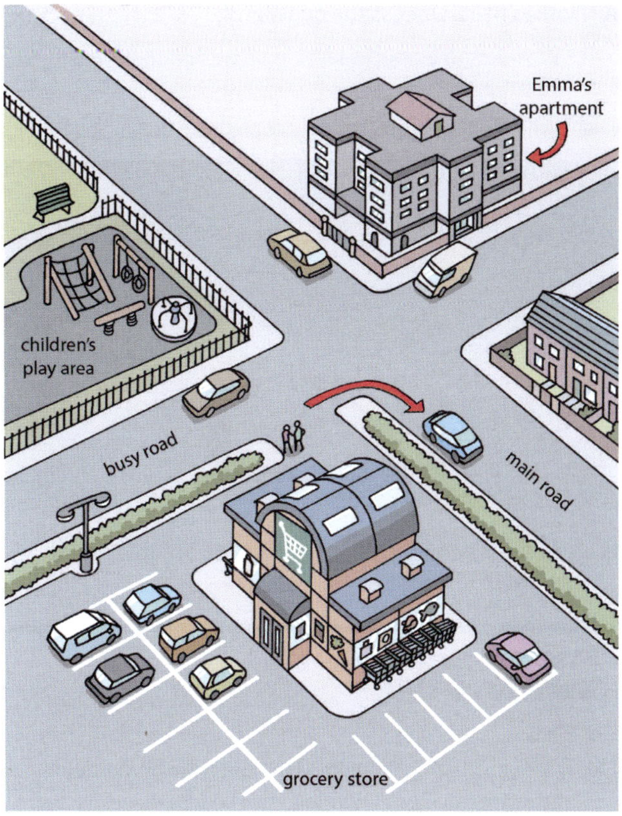

D Complete the sentences with *and*, *but*, *or*, *so* or *because*.

1 The air is dirty __________ there are too many cars.
2 There should be more parks for children __________ teenagers.
3 We shouldn't litter __________ play loud music.
4 We like the play area, __________ it's too small.
5 More children are living here, __________ the neighborhood should be safer.

WRITING

A PLAN You are going to write an email of complaint. Think of a problem in your neighborhood and two or more solutions to your problem.

B WRITE Write your email of complaint.

- Use Emma's email and the Writing skills box to help you.
- Check your writing for mistakes with grammar, vocabulary and spelling.

C REVIEW Work in groups. Read your emails and decide which one will be the most successful.

Write an email about a travel experience

W– ordering events

A Work in pairs. Discuss the questions.

1 Why do some people feel it is important to have a vacation?

2 What kind of problems do people have on vacation?

B Read Amal's email. Underline any of the problems you thought of in Exercise A.

To: Cleo
Subject: We're back!

Hi Cleo,

How are you? Thanks for feeding the cat. We're home, but there's no electricity, so I'm writing this on my phone. We had a terrible vacation. Scott broke his leg!

First, bad weather delayed our flight. We arrived at the chalet in the middle of the night, so the next morning we were really tired. After breakfast, we went to the ski lifts, but they were closed because it was too windy.

The following day, it wasn't so windy and we had a great time on the slopes in the morning. Then, we stopped for some lunch, but when I wanted to pay I couldn't find my wallet!

Two days later, the real disaster happened. We were skiing down a busy slope when Scott fell over and broke his leg. We had to fly to the local hospital in a helicopter. His leg is in a cast for the next six weeks.

I'll call you tomorrow.

Amal

C Read again and number the events in the order they happened (1–6).

___ Scott had an accident.
___ There was a problem at Amal's home.
_1_ The flight left the airport late.
___ It wasn't possible to go up the mountain.
___ Amal lost something.
___ The weather was better.

D Find and underline the words that helped you order the events. There are six words or phrases.

E Complete the sentences with the words in the box. Use the information in the box to help you.

Ordering events

When you write about an experience, use sequencing words and phrases like the ones you underlined in Amal's email to help readers follow the order of events.

after ~~first~~ hours morning next then

1 _First_, we missed the bus, so we had to take a taxi.

2 The following ________, I got the correct visa and crossed the border on foot.

3 The ________ day, we woke up to the sound of the ocean.

4 We drove for four hours, and ________ stopped for some lunch.

5 Two ________ later, my friend found her cell phone behind the couch.

6 ________ a quick lunch, we began walking again in the rain.

F Work in pairs. Cover Amal's email and retell the story using sequencing words and the events in Exercise C.

WRITING

A PLAN You are going to write an email to a friend about a good or bad travel experience. Think about the following:

1 Was it a good or bad experience?

2 Where were you and who were you with?

3 What happened?

4 How did the experience end?

B WRITE Write an email to a friend. Use the checklist to help you.

- ☐ I have written to a friend.
- ☐ I have started with an informal greeting and finished with an informal sign-off.
- ☐ I have used sequencing words and phrases to order the events.
- ☐ I have checked my spelling, vocabulary and grammar.

C REVIEW Work in pairs. Read your partner's email and ask questions about his/her experience.

4 Writing — Write an invitation and reply

W– informal emails

A Read Marta's message and answer the questions.

1 Why is Marta messaging her friends?
2 What kind of evening is she planning on Saturday?
3 What should her guests bring?

To: elviraandjan, ravi.gupta, stuart.jackson
Subject: Hygge Evening
Hi guys,
[1]How are things? Hope you're OK. [2]Life's good, but as usual, I'm looking forward to the weekend.
Actually, that is why I'm writing. [3]Are you doing anything on Saturday night? I'm planning a *hygge* evening around 7 pm at my place. [4]Can you make it?
I'm going to bake some cookies, light lots of candles and we could play a board game or watch a movie – or both! 😃
Anyway, [5]let me know whether you can come. All you need to bring is yourself, some warm socks and a wool sweater 😉
[6]It would be nice to see you.
Marta

B Look at Marta's message again. Match the underlined phrases (1–6) with the phrases with a similar meaning (a–f).

a Let me know if you're coming.
b Would you like to come?
c Everything is fine.
d Do you have any plans for …?
e How's life?
f I hope you can make it.

C Read two replies to Marta's message. Who is and is not coming to her *hygge* evening?

Dear Marta,
Nice to hear from you!
Thanks for inviting us on Saturday. We'd love to come, but we're going to Jan's parents' house for dinner, so I'm afraid we can't make it. I'm meeting them for the first time! I'm sure it will be fine, but I am a little nervous. Your *hygge* evening sounds much more relaxing!
Anyway, I'll let you know how it goes. Let's get together soon. I have so much to tell you.
See you soon,
Elvira

Hi Marta,
Long time no see. I hope you're well!
Thanks for the invitation for Saturday. A *hygge* evening sounds like just what I need, and I'd love to come. Who else will be there? Are Elvira and Jan coming?
Are you sure I can't bring any food? I could make some homemade snacks or something.
Let me know. It'll be gr8 to see you.
Love,
Ravi

D Read again and underline the phrases Marta's friends use to:

1 say thank you
2 say yes to the invitation
3 say no to the invitation
4 give a reason for saying no
5 mention the next time they'll meet

E Complete the box with words from the emails in Exercises A and C.

Informal emails

Start informal emails with a friendly greeting.
- *Dear Marta,*
- *Hi/Hello Marta,*
- *Hi* [1]______ (to a group; men, women or mixed)

Mention your last contact with other person.
- *Nice to hear from you.*
- *Long time no* [2]______ (when you haven't seen the person for a long time)

Use emoticons and abbreviations, but don't overuse them.
- *It'll be* [3]______ *to see you.*

Don't use full forms. Use contractions.
- *I hope ~~you are~~ you're well.*
- *We ~~would~~* [4]______ *love to come.*

Finish with a friendly goodbye.
- *Bye for now,*
- [5]______ *soon,*
- *Love,*

WRITING

A WRITE Work in pairs. You are organizing a party at your place. Write a message inviting another pair of students. Use Exercise E above to help you. Write 100–150 words.

B WRITE Swap messages with another pair of students and reply to their invitation. Use the Writing skills box to help you. Write 50–100 words. Include the following information:

- say thank you for the invitation
- say yes or no to the invitation (if no, give a reason)
- mention the next time you'll meet

W– beginning and ending emails and letters

English-speaking vacation nannies and mannies (job s632)

Vacation Hands agency is looking for English-speaking nannies and mannies (male nannies) to travel with families on their summer and winter vacations. You will take care of the children during the day and babysit in the evenings. Experience is an advantage. Good pay, plus all travel, accommodations and food included. Reply with a résumé and a copy of your passport to Olga Zatorska at ol.zator@vacationhands.nett

A Work in pairs. Read the advertisement. Would you or anyone you know be interested in this job? Why/Why not?

B Read Maurice's cover email. Do you think Maurice will be offered an interview? Why?

To: Ms. Zatorska
Subject: Vacation manny job

[1]Dear Ms. Zatorska,
[2]I am writing to apply for the job of vacation manny with the Vacation Hands agency. [3]I attached a copy of my résumé.
[4]Right now, I am studying at the University of Edinburgh and am available to work from July 1st to September 30th.
[5]I speak fluent English and Spanish and enjoy working with children. Last summer, I was an activities supervisor at a summer camp for 6–12-year-olds. My energy and creativity made me popular with the children. I believe this experience will be very useful. [6]A job with the Vacation Hands agency would be an exciting opportunity to learn new skills and work in an international environment.
[7]I look forward to hearing from you.
[8]Sincerely yours,
Maurice Garcia

C Read again. Put the different parts of a cover email in the correct order (1–7).

___ why you want this job
___ what you are doing now and when you are available
___ polite ending
___ reason for writing
_1_ a formal greeting
___ details about your experience and character
___ attachments, for example, your résumé

D Look at the box. Which beginnings and endings are formal (F)? Which are informal (I)?

Beginning and ending emails and letters

Beginning		Ending	
1 Hello,	_I_	7 See you soon,	___
2 Dear Sir/Madam,	___	8 Bye for now,	___
3 Dear all,	___	9 Lots of love,	___
4 Hi everyone,	___	10 Sincerely yours,	___
5 Dear Mr. Cox,	___	11 Yours truly,	___
6 Dear Diane,	___	12 Kind regards,	___
		13 Best wishes,	___

E Replace the underlined phrases in the email with similar phrases in the box.

Dear Sir/Madam, I am fluent in
I hope to hear from you soon.
I would like to apply for Please find attached
the knowledge and skills I developed there
Working for Yours truly,

F Work in pairs. What kind of skills, experience and personality would be helpful for this summer job?

Waiters and waitresses wanted (job h384)

Are you looking for part-time work? We need friendly, hard-working people to join our evening table service team at Blue Moon Asian Food Center. Experience is an advantage, but we will give full training. Attractive wages and free meals. Write with a résumé to noi.warumdee@mail.nett.

WRITING

A PLAN You are going to write a cover email to apply for the job in Writing Exercise F. Take notes for a cover email. Use Exercise C to help you.

B WRITE Write your cover email. Use the strategies in the box and Maurice's email to help you.

W– ordering information

A Read the product reviews from an online shopping website and match each review (1–3) with a picture (a–c).

a

b

c

1 **Really useful** ★★★★★
I bought this cool little device to help me get in shape, and **I'm very** [1] ___happy___ **with it**. It's comfortable and **I like the color**. It tells me how many steps I've taken, and how many calories I've burned each day. It also gives me information about how I slept. **It's very** [2] ________ and I find it motivates me to do more exercise than before. **It's made of** rubber, so it's waterproof and also very light. **It was definitely** [3] ________ **the money** and it arrived the day after I ordered it. [4] ________ **recommended** for anyone who is interested in health and fitness.

2 **Ouch!** ★★★☆☆
I bought this a few weeks ago to help me exercise. **It was a** [5] ________ **price** and it seems to be **well made. It was easy to put together** and **came with** a book full of different exercises to try. **The only** [6] ________ **is** it is really difficult to use! My stomach muscles aren't very strong and I find most of the exercises in the book impossible. I'm sure with enough practice it will get easier, but for now I have to say I don't look forward to using it. [7] ________ **for** those who don't mind the pain!

3 **Save your money** ★☆☆☆☆
My girlfriend bought me these as a birthday present, but **I was very** [8] ________ **with them**. Yes, **they look nice** and are comfortable to wear, but there's one big problem. **They are really** [9] ________ **quality.** I wore them in the gym once, and after about half an hour, I noticed there was a hole in the side. Obviously these were very **badly** [10] ________. I sent them back to the website and got a new pair, but after a few more trips to the gym … it happened again! **I don't recommend these** at all. They were **a real** [11] ________ **of money.**

B Read again. Complete the phrases in **bold** with the words in the box.

disappointed	highly	made	happy	poor	problem
reasonable	recommended	useful	waste	worth	

C Read again. Which phrases in **bold** describe positive things about the products, which describe negative and which are neutral?

I'm very happy with it. = positive

I was very disappointed with them. = negative

It's made of … = neutral

D Read the information in the box. Then read the reviews again and number the parts of a review in the correct order (1–4).

Ordering information

Think carefully about the order in which you present information in reviews and other types of factual writing. Organize your ideas into clear and logical paragraphs to make your writing easy for readers to follow.

negative points ___
recommendation (or not) ___
positive points ___
why you bought the product ___

E Work in pairs. Describe one product you have bought recently that you recommend and one that you do not.

WRITING

A PLAN Imagine you have bought one of the products below. Take notes on the following questions.

a pair of running sneakers

a fitness game for a game console

a winter sports jacket

a mountain bike

1 What positive points does the product have?
2 What negative points does the product have?

B WRITE Write a 100-word review of the product for a shopping website. Explain why you bought it and what positive and negative points it has. Then make a recommendation.

C REVIEW Work in groups. Read you classmates' reviews. Which are the best and worst products?

Irregular Verbs

Base form	Simple past	Past participle
be	was/were	been
become	became	become
begin	began	begun
break	broke	broken
bring	brought	brought
build	built	built
buy	bought	bought
can	could	(been able to)
catch	caught	caught
choose	chose	chosen
come	came	come
cost	cost	cost
cut	cut	cut
drink	drank	drunk
eat	ate	eaten
fall	fell	fallen
feel	felt	felt
find	found	found
forget	forgot	forgotten
get	got	got
give	gave	given
go	went	gone / been
grow	grew	grown
have	had	had
hear	heard	heard
hit	hit	hit
hold	held	held
hurt	hurt	hurt
keep	kept	kept
know	knew	known
leave	left	left
lend	lent	lent
let	let	let

Base form	Simple past	Past participle
lose	lost	lost
make	made	made
mean	meant	meant
meet	met	met
must	had to	(had to)
pay	paid	paid
put	put	put
read	read	read
ride	rode	ridden
run	ran	run
say	said	said
see	saw	seen
sell	sold	sold
send	sent	sent
set	set	set
shut	shut	shut
sing	sang	sung
sit	sat	sat
sleep	slept	slept
speak	spoke	spoken
spell	spelled	spelled
spend	spent	spent
stand	stood	stood
steal	stole	stolen
take	took	taken
teach	taught	taught
tell	told	told
think	thought	thought
throw	threw	thrown
understand	understood	understood
wear	wore	worn
win	won	won
write	wrote	written

PHONETIC SYMBOLS											
Single vowels			Diphthongs			Consonants					
/ɪ/	fish	/fɪʃ/	/uw/	new	/nuw/	/p/	pen	/pen/	/s/	snake	/sneɪk/
/iː/	bean	/biːn/	/eɪ/	face	/feɪs/	/b/	bag	/bæg/	/z/	zoo	/zuː/
/ʊ/	foot	/fʊt/	/ɔɪ/	boy	/bɔɪ/	/t/	tea	/tiː/	/ʃ/	shop	/ʃɒp/
/uː/	shoe	/ʃuː/	/oʊ/	nose	/noʊz/	/d/	dog	/dɒg/	/ʒ/	television	/'telɪvɪʒən/
/e/	egg	/eg/	/ju/	use	/juz/	/ʧ/	chip	/ʧɪp/	/m/	map	/mæp/
/ə/	mother	/'mʌðər/	/aɪ/	eye	/aɪ/	/ʤ/	jazz	/ʤæz/	/n/	name	/neɪm/
/ɜː/	word	/wɜːrd/	/aʊ/	mouth	/maʊθ/	/k/	cake	/keɪk/	/ŋ/	ring	/rɪŋ/
/ɔː/	talk	/tɔːk/				/g/	girl	/gɜːrl/	/h/	house	/haʊs/
/æ/	back	/bæk/				/f/	film	/fɪlm/	/l/	leg	/leg/
/ʌ/	bus	/bʌs/				/v/	verb	/vɜːrb/	/r/	road	/roʊd/
/ɑː/	arm	/ɑːrm/				/θ/	thing	/θɪŋ/	/w/	want	/wɒnt/
/ɒ/	top	/tɒp/				/ð/	these	/ðiːz/	/j/	yes	/jes/

Audio scripts

UNIT 1

Lesson 1.1, Listening, Exercise C

1.1 **P = Paul I = Isabelle**

P: Hello, and welcome to *Everyday Psychology*. I'm Paul Ross, and with me today is psychologist and expert on relationships, Isabelle Ackerman.

I: Hello, Paul. Hello, listeners.

P: Isabelle, today's topic is meeting new people. Now, we regularly meet new people at work or in our social lives, but it can be difficult to talk to someone we don't know. I mean, what do you say to a stranger at a party or a new colleague at the office? Is it OK to talk about some topics, but not others? Have you ever met someone new and had no idea what to talk about? Today, you have some advice to help us 'break the ice' and start conversations with new people.

I: Yes, I do. Let's begin with a very simple tip. When you meet someone new, start with a smile. A smile can help us feel more relaxed, but that's easy to forget when you feel nervous.

P: And of course a friendly face is easier to talk to.

I: Yes. A nice way to continue a conversation is to say something positive. You could talk about the place or situation you are in and then ask a question. For example, at a party, try 'Are you having fun?' or 'I love this music! What is your favorite band?' To a new person at work, you can say 'Oh, I'm glad it's lunchtime. How's your first day going?'

P: So no complaining about the boss!

I: Not at first, no. But it is good to ask about other people. For example, in a new group of students, ask 'Do you know our teacher?' or, at a wedding ceremony, 'Did you enjoy the ceremony?' or 'How do you know the happy couple? Were you at school together?' Don't be negative about other people because you don't know who they know.

P: Yes, that could be dangerous.

I: Interests and studies are always good, safe topics to talk about. Questions like 'What kind of music do you like?' or 'Where did you study?' are usually easy to answer. Remember, ask lots of questions and give lots of answers. A successful conversation is like a game of tennis!

P: It takes hours and makes you tired?

I: Very funny. When you feel more relaxed, ask some personal questions. 'Where are you from?', 'Are you married?' and 'Do you have children?' are good examples. But be careful. Don't discuss topics like religion or politics with someone you don't know.

P: Some great tips. Isabelle, thank you very much. That's all for this week. Remember, many great friends meet after a smile and a simple 'hello'. Good luck breaking the ice and meeting new people. Please join us for the next episode of *Everyday Psychology* – we'll be discussing the hot topic …

UNIT 2

Lesson 2.2, Listening, Exercise B

2.2 **P = Presenter R = Richard**

P: More and more of the world's young people are going home to live with their parents after college. Why? And what is it like living at home again as an adult? How do parents feel about the situation? Today, we talk to members of 'the boomerang generation' and their parents about the advantages and disadvantages of living together again. Let's start with Richard …

R: I'm Richard Woodman, from the US. I'm 25 years old and at the moment, I'm living at home with my mom and dad. I … uh … graduated two years ago, but I'm still looking for a permanent job. I love my parents, but we … um … well, they are difficult to live with. We argue about the rules all the time. I'm sleeping in my old room and living with the people who took me to the park when I was little! I know I'm lucky to be here, but it's … you know … it isn't easy.

Lesson 2.2, Listening, Exercise C

2.3 **P = Presenter R = Richard G = Gordon A = Alice C = Carla**

P: More and more of the world's young people are going home to live with their parents after college. Why? And what is it like living at home again as an adult? How do parents feel about the situation? Today, we talk to members of 'The boomerang generation' and their parents about the advantages and disadvantages of living together again. Let's start with Richard …

R: I'm Richard Woodman, from the US. I'm 25 years old and at the moment, I'm living at home with my mom and dad. I … uh … graduated two years ago, but I'm still looking for a permanent job. I love my parents, but we … um … well, they are difficult to live with. We argue about the rules all the time. I'm sleeping in my old room and living with the people who took me to the park when I was little! I know I'm lucky to be here, but it's … you know … it isn't easy.

G: My name is Gordon Woodman. I'm Richard's dad. Of course, Richard's mom and I are, well, we're happy he is staying with us … most of the time. We're his parents and he can always rely on us, but we uh … we hope he finds the right job and, well, moves out as soon as possible. I want to make his bedroom into my home office. And his music, it's … well you know, thump, thump, thump all day and night. It drives me crazy! Anyway, we think he needs to be more independent. We love him, but he's unhappy, and he isn't learning about adult life living here with us.

A: Hi, I'm Alice Melo from Philadelphia, in the US. I'm 28 years old and I graduated last year. I work as a dentist and, at the moment, I'm living with my parents to save money for my own place. Well, I'm trying to save money anyway, ha ha! I studied in Colorado, but I … uh … couldn't find a job there, so, you know, I came back home. More and more of my friends are moving back home. It's great! Mom cooks and does all my laundry. She won't take any money from me … I tried, but … uh … so I'm not paying any bills. Of course, I help … sometimes … I help with the housework and the yard, I mean, now and again, you know. One day, I will do something special to thank them.

C: I'm Carla Melo, Alice's mom. We're very happy our daughter is home again. She's working hard and she wants to get her own place, but I always tell her she can live here with us forever! She's an adult now, I know, but she's still my baby! This year, my husband is traveling a lot for work, for his job, you know, so I'm very happy Alice is here with me. I don't like being on my own. I can talk to her, and she can save money and enjoy her mom's cooking.

UNIT 3

Lesson 3.2, Listening, Exercise C

3.4 **C = Chloe M = Matt**

C: Welcome to this week's *Amazing Adventures* podcast. I'm Chloe Cole, and with me is sailor and survival expert Matt Cabral. This week, the amazing story of the Robertson family and how they survived a month lost at sea in the Pacific Ocean.

In 1970, Dougal and Lyn Robertson and their four children were living on a farm in northern England. One ordinary day, Neil, one of their ten-year-old twins, said he wanted to leave the farm and sail around the world. Most families would probably laugh and say 'don't be silly', but the Robertsons saw the chance for an adventure. They sold their business, bought a boat, and on January 27th, 1971, started their journey across the Atlantic. Matt, what do you think of their decision?

M: Incredible. I mean, Dougal was an experienced sailor, but it was still a brave decision. Maybe not very sensible, but definitely brave!

C: Ha ha, yes. Well, sensible or not, the Robertsons made it across the Atlantic safely in their 13-meter boat, *The Lucette*. But on June 15th, 1972, while they were sailing out into the Pacific Ocean, things started to go very wrong.

Their boat was passing the Galapagos Islands when they noticed something large in the water behind them. It was a group of killer whales swimming toward the boat. Douglas, the eldest son, has said that when he saw the whales, he thought they were going to kill and eat the family. Well, the whales hit and sank their boat, but amazingly, the Robertsons all made it onto their small life raft, scared, but alive. I mean, they were very unlucky, weren't they, Matt?

M: Yes, they were. On average, there are only two to three accidents with boats and whales per year. But believe it or not, it wasn't all bad. I mean, first, the whales didn't eat them.

C: Ha! That's true.

M: And the life raft and another very small wooden boat survived the accident. And luckily they were carrying some water, some dry bread, cookies, a bag of onions and some fruit in the life raft.

C: Yes, but after six days, all the food was gone, so they collected rainwater to drink, and killed turtles and ate the meat and drank the blood. Then, 17 days after the accident, their life raft failed and they had to move to their wooden boat. It was called *The Ednamair* and was only three meters long. Can you imagine the whole family in that small boat?

M: It sounds like an impossible situation. You have to be strong and stay positive to survive something like this. There was only one dry seat in the boat, so most of the time they were sitting in water. But they didn't give up hope.

C: And finally, 38 days after the accident, a Japanese fishing boat found them and took them to dry land and safety.

M: It's an incredible story of survival.

C: Yes, it is. And now, Douglas Robertson works as an accountant in London, and amazingly, he has said that he actually enjoyed the family's adventure!

UNIT 4

Lesson 4.1, Listening, Exercise B

4.1 **S = Sylvia G = Greg**

S: Greggy! Ohhhhhh! It's so nice to see you!

G: Hi, Syl. Give me a hug. It's nice to see you, too … Do you have to call me Greggy?

S: Ha ha. Yes, and I'm going to introduce you to all my new friends as 'Greggy'. Was the trip OK?

G: Sure, sure. Mom gave me a ride to the station. She sends her love. She misses her darling daughter et cetera, et cetera. She's gonna call later.

S: Oh, good. How's Claire? Are you two OK? Still madly in love?

G: Oh, yeah, you know. Lucky girl.

S: Stop it.

G: She wanted to come this weekend, but tomorrow evening she's having dinner with some old friends. They arranged it a long time ago.

S: Of course. Never mind. Hopefully she'll make it next time. I have so many plans for us this weekend! It's such a great city. I can't wait to show you around. Are you hungry?

G: Always.

S: Yep, silly question. Let's go for lunch.

G: Wow, this place is cool.

S: Nice, right? I hang out with my friends here a lot. I think I'm going to bring Mom and Dad here, too … if they ever come and visit!

G: Ha! They will. And then they'll never leave!

S: Ha!

G: So, what are all these plans you have for us then?

S: Well, when we've finished lunch, I'm gonna text Angie and Mark and tell them to come and meet us, and we're going to go for a walk and show you the city center. Then we're meeting Duncan and Alicia at three o'clock, and I think we're going for coffee somewhere, but I'm not sure where.

G: Duncan and Alicia?

S: Oh, they're great. You'll like Duncan. He's a little like you.

G: What, handsome and intelligent?

S: Uhh … more like he's always thinking about his next meal.

G: I like him already.

S: After that, we're going to the market to look around; it's a beautiful old building, and we're going to do some food shopping because Duncan is making a curry dish for us all tonight. He's a great cook. Alicia says she and Duncan are going to open a restaurant one day. Anyway, …

G: Sounds great.

S: OK, so then tonight, we're going to the theater.

G: The theater?

S: Yes, I have tickets for a Shakespeare play.

G: What?

S: Ha ha! Only joking. We're seeing a comedy show. One of my friends is filming the show and he got us some free tickets.

G: Phew. That's more like it. What a great day you have planned, Syl! I can't wait.

S: And that's just today. Wait until you hear about tomorrow … In the morning, we're …

G: Uh, Syl, hang on. Did you hear that?

S: What?

G: Listen!

S: What? Is it the music?

G: No … no … it's … I think … yes, it's the sound of my empty stomach. Are we getting something to eat, or what?

S: Pfffft. You and your stomach. Pass me a menu …

UNIT 5

Lesson 5.3, Listening, Exercise B

5.6 **G = Gemma B = Barry**

G: Good morning. You must be Barry. I'm Gemma.

B: Oh mmmm hmmfff … sorry. I'm just finishing my sandwich!

G: That's OK … Egg sandwich, is it?

B: Uh … Yes, egg. Sorry. My favorite. Nice to meet you, Emma.

G: It's Gemma.

B: Excuse me?

G: It's Gemma, not Emma.

B: Sorry! What a terrible start.

G: Please don't worry, Barry. Gemma Lockwood. Base One IT Services. I work in Human Resources. Sorry we're a little delayed today. Have you been here long?

B: Actually, I've been here since 9 am.

G: You've been here for … three hours?

B: Yes, well, I didn't want to be late. That's why I was hungry.

G: OK … well … uh … good! Come in and have a seat.

B: Thanks.

G: So, Barry, we are looking for people to work at our head office on the customer service team. First, could you tell me a little about yourself?

B: Ha ha. OK. Well, I'm Barry. I'm uh … 23 years old. Single, male, blond hair. Rather nervous in interviews … ha. I uh … I'm one meter tall, I have a cat named Yoda and I love … uh … egg sandwiches, ha ha, and … um … computers and … wait, did I just say one meter tall? Ha ha sorry. Uh … I'm one meter and seventy centimeters tall, and I …

G: Uh … Barry, maybe we could focus on your work experience. You work for a telemarketing company at the moment, is that right? How long have you worked there?

B: Uh, well, I left my old job in June … and now it's … well, I … I've worked at the call center for six weeks. Have you read my résumé? I did send one. I mean, I wrote everything there, so …

G: Uh … yes, but … tell me more. For example, why do you want to change jobs and work for Base One?

B: Oh, well, that's easy; I hate my job at the call center! I sit on the phone all day long asking people questions and nobody wants to talk to me. People get really angry and sometimes, well, they hang up the phone.

G: I … see. Uh … So, what do you know about Base One?

B: About what? OH! Yes … well … I'm … I think it's … could you repeat the question, please?

G: Uh … well … OK. What do you know about Base One IT Services?

B: Um, well Base One is a … great IT company, with … great services … and the office here is … um … really cool. And, you seem very nice, and I …

G: Barry, ahem! Teamwork is very important for us here at Base One. Can you tell me about a time when you worked as part of a team?

B: Um, you mean a real example?

G: Uh, yes.

B: Let me think … uhh, I … um, actually … uhh …

G: Um … OK. It says on your résumé that you enjoy skydiving. Wow! How long have you been interested in that?

B: Oh, well. I've liked skydiving since I was a teenager. It just looks so exciting! I've always wanted to try it.

G: So you haven't actually tried skydiving?

B: Well, I really want to.

G: And French poetry?

B: What?

G: Your résumé says you enjoy French poetry.

B: Does it? Oh yes! That's right. Of course, French poetry – love it.

G: Uh, Barry, I, uh, I think we've finished for today.

B: Oh, great – that was quick.

G: Yes, uh … do you uh … do you have any questions?

B: Um … No! No, I don't!

G: OK, so thanks again and … please don't call us … we … uh, we'll contact you. Thank you, Barry.

B: No, thank YOU, Emma.

UNIT 6

Lesson 6.1, Listening, Exercise C

6.1 **P = Pippa DS = Doctor Singh M = Michael DT = Doctor Tremblay L = Lia**

P: G'day, Australia! Pippa Chan on chatfmmelbourne.nett. Today, we are talking about health myths.

Half an hour on the internet leaves most people pretty confused about what's good for their health and what isn't. You know, one article says 'you drink too much coffee, but you don't drink enough water', then the next says coffee is good for you, but too much water is dangerous! Confusing? Very!

I mean, let's say you are one of the many people who goes through life feeling tired a lot of the time. If you look online, you'll find one expert that says 'you don't sleep enough' and another that says 'you sleep too much'. Ha! And if you can't sleep? Oh, it's because you go to bed too early. No, no, no it's because you don't go to bed early enough! And of course EVERYthing makes you fat.

So how do we know what to believe? Well, we've been down to Melbourne City Hospital to ask some medical professionals about the reality behind some common health myths. Let's hear from the experts …

DS: Hi. I'm Dr. Singh and I work at Melbourne City Hospital. My myth concerns how much water we need to drink. Most people have probably heard that not drinking enough water can cause headaches. And they are right – that isn't a myth. But many of us have probably also heard that we need to drink eight glasses of water per day to stay healthy – well, that isn't exactly true. The eight glasses, or around two liters, includes all liquids: tea, coffee, juice, et cetera – plus the water you get from food, which is around one fifth of your daily total. So how much water should we drink? Well, my advice is drink when you are thirsty and you'll be OK.

M: Hi, my name is Michael. I'm a nurse here in Melbourne. Many people believe that eating fatty food makes them fat, but in fact, that isn't the whole truth. Eating more calories than you need makes you fat. Yes, it's true that fat has lots of calories, but so do carbohydrates and sugars. It isn't actually too much fat that makes you fat, it's too many calories. Some fat is necessary, so you can still enjoy your burger as part of a balanced diet. And to burn those extra calories? Get up off that couch and get moving!

DT: Hi, I'm Dr. Tremblay from Canada. The Australian winter is here and so are colds and flu. You remember Grandma's advice … 'Hat! Scarf! Keep warm, or you'll catch a cold.' Well, Australia isn't as cold as Canada, but it is sensible to make sure you're warm enough. However, the truth is that cold weather doesn't cause colds and flu. They are caused by viruses. You are more likely to catch a cold inside, where there are lots of people. And remember, if you have a cold and are suffering with a headache, a cough or a sore throat, get plenty of rest, drink warm drinks – unless you have a temperature – and make sure you are getting enough vitamins. Don't take antibiotics! They don't kill viruses and they won't help a cold.

L: Hi, I'm Lia. I'm a medical student from London and I want to talk about eggs! Some people believe that you shouldn't eat more than one or two eggs a week. This is probably because of old advice. In the past, the warning was always 'too many eggs are bad for your heart', but we now know that an egg or two per day doesn't increase the risk of heart disease in healthy people. Egg-cellent news for egg lovers – Egg-xactly what they wanted to hear! Ha ha – sorry!

P: Wow! Thank you to all our egg-sperts. Interesting stuff! We'll be back with music from Enrique Egg-lesias after the break.

Notes

Macmillan Education
4 Crinan Street
London N1 9XW
A division of Macmillan Education Limited

Companies and representatives throughout the world

American Language Hub Level 2A Student's Book ISBN 978-1-380-04708-3
American Language Hub Level 2A Student's Book with Student's App
ISBN 978-1-380-04702-1

Written by Daniel Brayshaw and Jon Hird
With thanks to Edward Price and Carol Goodwright for additional authoring and to Signature Manuscripts for the Grammar Hub pages.

First published 2020

Designed by emc design ltd
Illustrated by Peter Lubach, Rasmus Juul, Rose Frith represented by Lemonade Illustration
Cover design by Restless
Cover image by Getty Images/Linghe Zhao
Picture research by Emily Taylor and Victoria Gaunt
Café Hub videos produced by Creative Listening
Café Hub video scripts written by James and Luke Vyner

Authors' acknowledgements

Daniel Brayshaw would like to thank the whole team for their invaluable support. Also, a special thanks to Sue Kay and Vaughan Jones for all their advice and guidance, and to my wife, Lucyna Brayshaw, for everything. Last but not least to Flash, our dog, for insisting I take regular breaks from the desk. Good boy.

Jon Hird would like to thank the Macmillan Education Editorial team for their input, ideas and hard work in shaping the content of the book.

The authors and publishers would like to thank the following for permission to reproduce their photographs:

Alamy Action Plus Sports Images pXX(4), Ian Allenden pXXVII, Alvey & Towers Picture Library p29(tr), Roger Cracknell 01/classic pXXVI, Cultura p42(ken), XXIV, Deymos Photo pXXIX(c), GeoPic p22, Incamerastock p13(cl), jvphoto p52(9), NakoPhotography p42(bret), Alexandre Rotenberg p12(r), Michiel Vaartjes pXIX(4); **Bananastock** p69 (background); **BrandX** pXVIII(3); **Corbis** pp36(tl), 53(1),102(3); **Fancy** p56(1); **Getty Images** pp17(a), 28-29(background), 42(lena), 47, 48-49(background), 52(3), 52(5), 52(10), XVIII(2, 4,5,f,g,h), XIX(1,2), AFP/Timothy A Clary p51, AFP/John Macdougall p34(tl), AFP/Justin Tallis p44, Age footstock pp13(bl), 16(clocks), Ajr images p42(helen), Altrendo p17(d), Jacob Ammentorp Lund p33, Sally Anscombe pp17(c), AYImages pXXIX(cl), Baiterek Media pp36(b), 37(b), XX(l), Jonny Baker p18(b), Scott Barbour p56(b), Thomas Barwick p55(tl), Katarzyna Bialasiewicz p52(7), Blend Images pp14, XVIII(e), pXXIII(bmr), Suphawinee Boonpeng p52(br), Caiaimage/Paul Bradbury pXXVIII(l), Adrienne Bresnahan p39(cr), Petar Chernaev p34(tr), China Photos p41, Chombosan p35, Aurora Creative pXX(8), Cultura pp56(5), XX(8), XXIII(bcr), Jake Curtis p32, DaveLongMedia pXIX(7), Sofie Delauw p15, domin_domin pXXIX(bl), DNY59 p58(br), Dorling Kindersley p28(br), Karin Dreyer p59(toothache),E+, iStockphoto/Eshma pXXIX(br), FatCamera pXXIX(cr), Antonio de Moraes Barros Filho P62(d), Fizkes p59(bad back), FotografiaBasica p58-59(background), Franckreporter pp19, 18-19(background), fstop123 p39(br), Mitchell Funk pXX(7), Vladimir Godnik p59(headache), GretaMarie p48(b), Haag & Kropp p49(br), Izabela Habur pp36(tcr), Hero Images pp2, 54(br), Rolf Hicker p25(bl), Hindustan Times p55(bl), Andrew Hounslea p52(bl), The Image Bank pp42(t), 56(6), XX(6), Image Source pp52(8), XVIII(1), Chase Jarvis pXX(1), Jokic pXXVIII(r), Kozorog p36(tcl), Alexander Kuguchin p26(inset), Jason Langley p52(bcl), Loop Images p31, MariusFM77 p56(2), Michael Marquand p59(br), Maximilian Stock Ltd p52(bcr), Mervana p30(travel icons), Stuart Miller pXVIII(g), Monkeybusinessimages p4(cr), Dean Mouhtaropoulos p54(t), Naumoid pXIX(6), Nikada p13(cm), OJO Images pp52(4), 59(stomache ache), XXIII(br), Andrew Olney p16(inset), Omgimages pXVIII(d), Rudy Orozco P8(croissants), Perspectives p1, Zoltan Polgar p56(3), Querbeet pXIX(3), Ranplett p38-39(background), Alex Raths p17(b), RICOWde p23, Science Photo Library p8-9(background), Jordan Siemens p21, SIphotography p53(2), James Steidl pXIX(5), Sundown100 p26-27(b), Svetikd p36(tr), B. Tanaka p11, Tom And Steve p52(6), Shomos Uddin p8(bl), Umbertoleporini p12(l), Universal Images Group pp59(sore toe), Betsie Van der Meer pp7, XX(3), Vkuslandia p56(4), Fabian Wentzel p43, Westend61 p46(b), XiXinXing pXVIII(h), William R. Sallaz/Getty Images pXX(2); **IMAGE 100** p40; **Image Source** pp52(tl,tcl), XVIII(c); **Mihaela Noroc** p4-5; **Photodisc** pXVIII(b); **Robertson Family Archive** pp24(bl,br), 25(br); **Shutterstock**/Mark & Anna Wilson pXXIII(bmr); **Thinkstock** pp52(tr),XVIII(a),XX(5); **123RF** Mile Atanasov pXXIX(a,b).

Printed and bound in Mexico
by Compañía Editorial Ultra, S.A. de C.V.

2021 2020
04 03 02 01

Commissioned photographs in the Café Hubs by Creative Listening.

The authors and publishers are grateful for permission to reprint the following copyright material:

p36 Helliwell, J., Layard, R., & Sachs, J. (2016). World Happiness Report 2016. New York: Sustainable Development Solutions Network; p42 Extract from 'One in five children just want to be rich when they grow up' by Keith Perry. Originally published in The Telegraph, 5 August 2014. © Telegraph Media Group Limited 2014. Reprinted with permission of The Telegraph.